OXFORDS
RAMBI

Other counties in this series include:

Avon	Hertfordshire
Bedfordshire	Kent
Buckinghamshire	Middlesex
Cambridgeshire	Somerset
Dorset	Suffolk
East Sussex	Surrey
Essex	West Sussex
Gloucestershire	Wiltshire

Other Walking Guides available from Countryside Books

Exploring the Pilgrims' Way
Exploring the Ridgeway
Walks Around the Downs
New Forest Walks
Short Walks in the New Forest
The Test Way
The Wayfarers Walk
New Forest Companion
In the Steps of Jane Austen
In the Steps of Thomas Hardy

OXFORDSHIRE RAMBLES

Fourteen Country Walks around Oxfordshire

Nick Channer

With Historical Notes

COUNTRYSIDE BOOKS
NEWBURY, BERKSHIRE

First Published 1990

COUNTRYSIDE BOOKS
3 Catherine Road
Newbury, Berkshire

ISBN 1 85306 071 2

Sketch maps by Pip Challenger

Cover photograph: View over Goring
taken by Andy Williams

Produced through MRM Associates Ltd, Reading
Typeset by Robert Antony Ltd, Ringwood, Hants
Printed in England by J. W. Arrowsmith Ltd., Bristol

Introduction

The county of Oxfordshire has an interesting and varied landscape. As well as the well known picturesque villages and towns along the Thames there is much more to delight the rambler.

In the south-west the county meets Berkshire high on the Downs, offering open vistas and links with the past along the ancient Ridgeway. The countryside in the north is much softer, with the honey-coloured cottages and sparkling rivers of the Cotswolds, and historic Banbury offering a gateway to the Midland counties. By way of contrast the south-east corner provides opportunities to explore the colourful beechwoods of the Chiltern Hills. Not far from the dreaming spires of Oxford itself is the desolate landscape of Otmoor, a wilderness which seems curiously out of place.

The circular walks in this book offer a taste of these contrasting areas. They range in length from 3 to 8 miles. Details are given about the location of each walk. For those who like to break their walk for refreshment the names of pubs providing meals and other places selling food along or near the route are mentioned.

The sketch map that accompanies each walk is designed to guide walkers to the starting point and give a simple but accurate idea of the route to be taken. For those who like the benefit of detailed maps the relevant Ordnance Survey series sheets 1:50,000 are recommended.

The historical notes at the end of each chapter are designed to provide basic information about the places of interest along the route.

No special equipment is needed to enjoy the countryside on foot, but do wear a stout pair of shoes and remember that at least one muddy patch is likely even on the sunniest day. Please remember the Country Code and make sure gates are not left open nor any farm animals disturbed.

I hope you will gain as much enjoyment from these walks as I did in preparing them.

Nick Channer
March 1990

Contents

Acknowledgements

My grateful thanks to Sarah Ambler for her illustrations and to my walking companions Ian Knapp, David Jeffery and Simon Corbett who all agreed that a drink or two consumed in an Oxfordshire Inn made the effort of undertaking the walk that much more acceptable.

'Away, away from men and towns,
To the wild wood and the downs —
To the silent wilderness
Where the soul need not repress
Its music lest it should not find
An echo in another's mind,
While the touch of Nature's Art
Harmonises heart to heart.'

Shelley

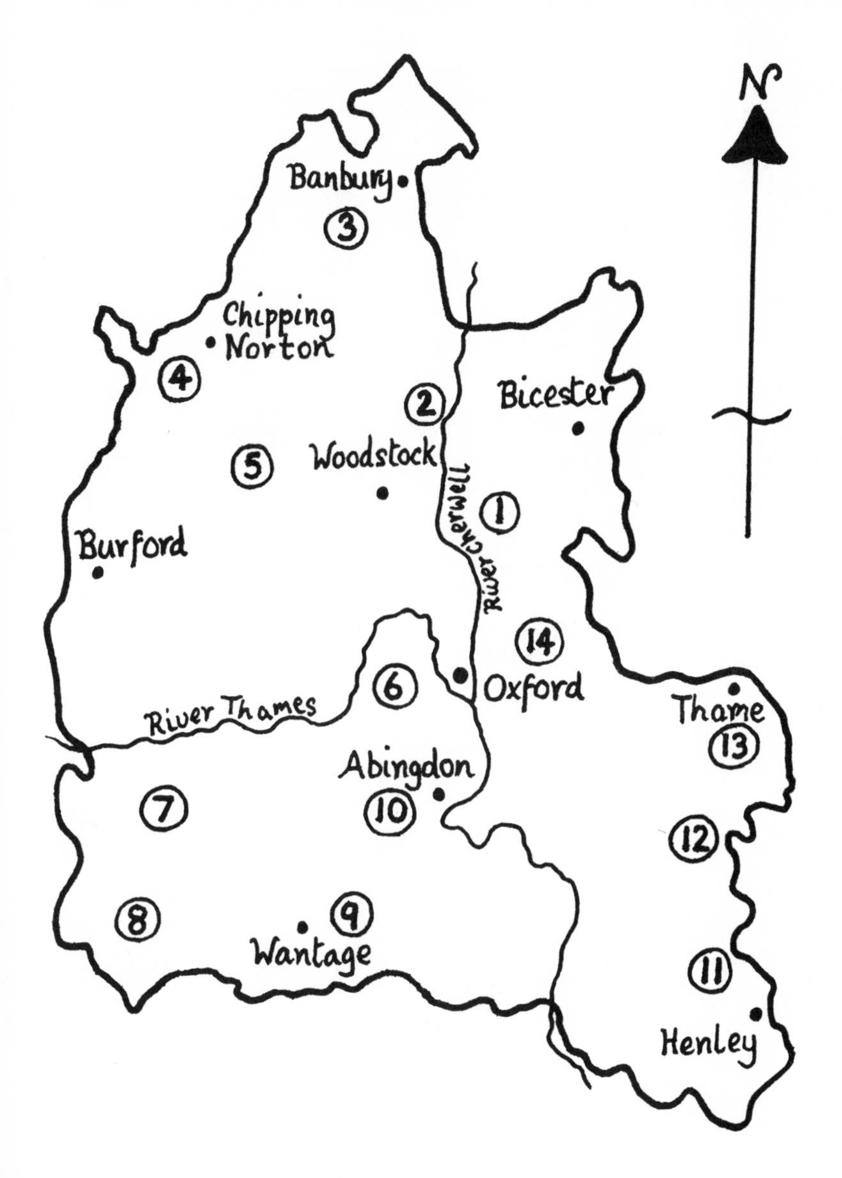

Sketch Map showing the locations of the walks

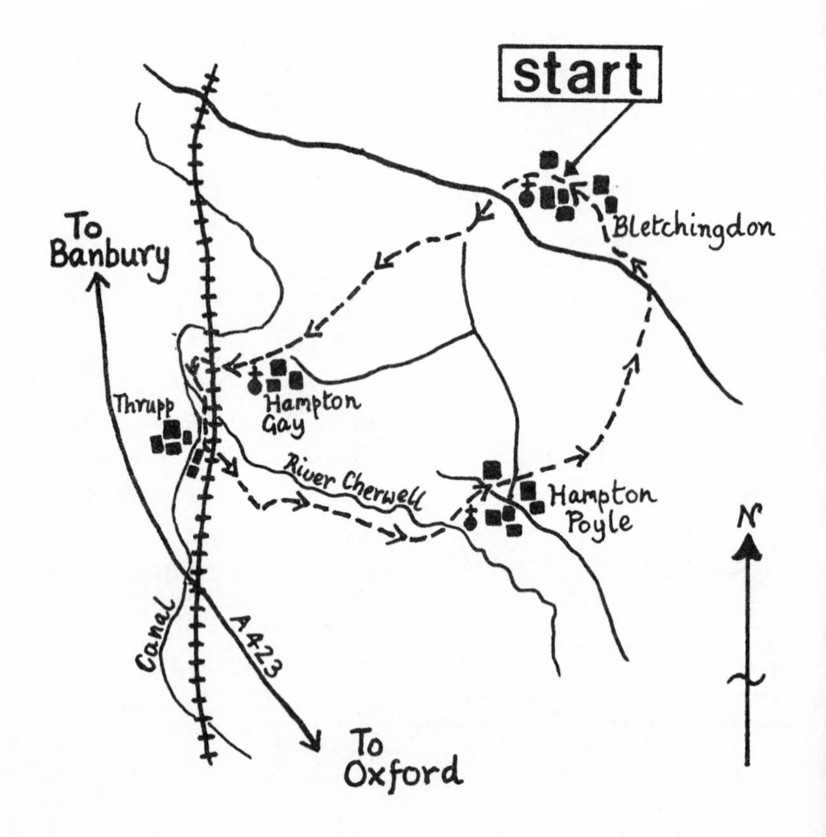
start
Bletchingdon
To
Banbury
Thrupp
Hampton
Gay
River Cherwell
Hampton
Poyle
N
Canal
A423
To
Oxford

WALK ONE

The Oxford Canal and the River Cherwell

Introduction: Beginning in Bletchingdon the walk crosses rolling windswept countryside to reach Hampton Gay. A few cottages, a church standing alone in the fields and the ruins of an old manor house are all that remain of this once thriving community which went into decline after disaster struck in the 19th century. The air of sadness surrounding Hampton Gay is quickly forgotten, however, when you reach Thrupp, a bright bustling canalside village a mile further on. The Oxford Canal here is often jammed with quaint colourful narrow boats, creating a zestful romantic scene. The final part of the walk is a pleasant stroll beside the banks of the Cherwell as far as Hampton Poyle and then across peaceful farmland passing the entrance to Bletchingdon Park.

Distance: The walk is about 6 miles and should be completed in about 3 hours.

Refreshments: The Black's Head in Bletchingdon offers coffee and food and has a garden. The Boat Inn at Thrupp provides hot and cold food and also includes a garden. The Bell at Hampton Poyle does bar snacks.

How to get there: Heading north from Oxford, as you approach Kidlington take the A43 road signposted Bicester. Turn left after about 3 miles signposted Bletchingdon. Park anywhere in the vicinity of the village green.

The Walk: Make for the southern corner of the village and take the road opposite, signposted Hampton Poyle. Walk along the road passing St Giles on the right and, on reaching the end of a line of houses on the left by the 30 mph speed restriction sign, bear right and head diagonally across the field towards several barns. Pass just to the right of them then begin to swing left towards a gate in the left-hand fence. Once through the gate go diagonally right across the field aiming for the left-hand edge of the trees. As you approach the gate leading into the next field look for a stile a few yards to the left and pass over it.

Cross the field roughly in a straight line and watch out for an arrow in the boundary to the right of some trees and bushes. Along this stretch there are good forward views to the west in the direction of Oxford Airport and Woodstock. In addition there are several other distinctive local landmarks to look out for: the tall spire of Kidlington church justly proud and visible for miles around, and over to the right a cement works. On reaching the arrow cross over the wooden fence into the field then descend the slope by keeping to the left-hand boundary. Bear right in the field corner and then after a few yards pass through the gate on the left with an accompanying arrow. Head straight across the field towards the farm buildings at Hampton Gay (HN). Go through the gate and then turn right, following the little lane as it runs between the buildings of Manor Farm on the left and a row of cottages on the right. On reaching the gate continue ahead into the field following the straight track.

Over to the right there are the ruined remains of the old Manor House and a short distance beyond it, yet isolated from the rest of the village, undiscovered in its lonely farmland setting is St Giles church. In order to visit the church or at least to gain a closer look at it, turn right across the field and make for the main gate. If the door is locked the keys can be obtained from Manor Farm or Manor Cottage nearby. On leaving the churchyard head for the stile and once over it cross with care the main London, Oxford and Midlands railway line. Immediately you are across the line pass over another stile and then head across a meadow, aiming for a smattering of trees and bushes. On reaching them look out for a bridge slightly to your right taking you across the meandering waters of the river Cherwell to a stile. Continue ahead through the trees and bushes towards a gate. Go through it and follow the track but make sure you leave it immediately before the bridge by bearing left onto the towpath of the Oxford Canal. Very shortly the church at Shipton-on-Cherwell suddenly looms large, looking down on you from its distinctive canalside position over on the opposite bank.

Continue along the towpath to Thrupp (HN). To reach The Boat Inn follow the path sharp right and then cross the bridge to the opposite towpath. Keep to the road on the right-hand bank passing a row of attractive stone cottages. Just beyond them on the right is The Boat Inn.

Suitably rested and refreshed return to the canal bridge, cross it and continue ahead to the right of the Thrupp Maintenance Yard sign. Pass to the right of some thatched cottages by keeping to the track and head towards the railway line. Follow the track through the tunnel and then cross a stile leading into a field. The path heads across the field towards a line of trees and bushes and in a minute or two the river Cherwell comes into view a few yards away on the left. Pass into the next field and continue ahead. At length the path reaches the field boundary. Cross a wooden footbridge over the ditch and continue as the path runs up hard by the edge of the Cherwell, the river winding in snake-like fashion through the countryside.

Continue along the grassy path, through the gap in the hedge into the next field and on beside the river or near to it. The magnificent 15th century spire of Kidlington church rises above the landscape along this stretch of the walk, serving as a very useful landmark for those a little unsure of their bearings.

Draw alongside the river, go through another gap and continue ahead. Pass through a kissing gate into the next field. Soon the buildings of Manor Farm come into view a short distance away on the opposite bank of the river. On reaching the concrete bridge over the Cherwell, cross it and then proceed diagonally right across the field towards a stile in the next boundary. Cross it and follow the path along the left-hand edge of the field. In the field corner swing right and after a few yards turn left onto a path between a wire fence and a stone wall. The path graduates to a track on the outskirts of Hampton Poyle. Follow it to the road and then turn right and walk along Church Lane to the junction in the centre of the village.

The Bell Inn is within sight at this stage — situated a short distance further along the road ahead of you on the left. From the Bell return to this road junction and swing right into Bletchingdon Road. Beyond the line of houses on the right, turn right onto a cart track and follow it as it heads in an easterly direction with a hedge on the right and open fields on the left. Pass a small pond on the right and soon the track bears right into the next field and then swings left, keeping close to the left-hand boundary. Cross the next field boundary and continue ahead with the hedge on the left.

Follow the track as it swings right and then left. Cross the next field, this time with the boundary on the right. At the next boundary turn left onto a narrow path running along the edge of the field. Follow the path with the hedge on the left into the field corner; cross a wooden footbridge over a stream and continue into the next field which is narrow and rather elongated in shape. Keep over towards the left boundary and at length the path joins the road through a gap in the hedge.

Turn left here and immediately pass the entrance to Diamond Farm Caravan site on the left. Proceed along the road and after about a ¼ mile there is a gap in the hedge and undergrowth on the right. Pass through it and enter the field beyond. Cross the field by going diagonally left towards the distant gate. Pass through it and follow the path between two ponds taking care as the ground here can be extremely wet and boggy. Cross the footbridge followed by a fence and then head left along the left field boundary. In the field corner turn left over the fence, cross the footbridge and then another fence and continue along the right-hand edge of the field. In the corner pass through a gate and proceed ahead with an area of woodland on the left. Pass through the meadow with distant glimpses of Bletchingdon's houses and bungalows over on the right. There are spectacular backward views of distant downland topped with trees over towards Otmoor and the Chilterns as you reach the top of the slope. In the upper part of the field pass through the gate and out into the road.

Turn left and walk back towards the village centre. As you bear left near the 30mph speed limit sign it is worth taking a small detour to look at Bletchingdon Park (HN) on the northern outskirts of the village. On this bend turn right through a kissing gate and follow the path through the park as far as the church. Return by the same route to the road and continue ahead to the village green where the walk began.

Historical Notes

Hampton Gay: The old village has long been abandoned but once it was a prosperous place and by the second half of the 19th century there was a productive paper mill here. However, a major train disaster in December 1874 on the nearby stretch of track seemed to mark the start of the village's downfall.

It was Christmas Eve and there was heavy snow on the ground. A train from Paddington bound for the Midlands acquired an extra coach at Oxford to help cope with the large numbers of passengers travelling home for Christmas. As the train headed north out of Oxford a wheel-tire on the additional coach broke. Almost at once the final carriages left the rails. The rest of the train continued for some distance and then plunged down the embankment beside the Cherwell. Thirty passengers died in the disaster — regarded at that time as the worst in railway history. The injured and dying were taken to the Manor House, the mill and other homes in the area. Queen Victoria sent a message of sympathy.

It was the saddest Christmas the village had ever known. But there was further sorrow to come. In 1887 the fine 16th century Manor House was ravaged by fire and the adjoining paper mill closed down. The village never really recovered from this catalogue of tragedy and today the size of Hampton Gay is about the same as it was in medieval times. St Giles church, unlike the Manor House, is still intact. It was built in 1767 though some sources suggest the tower dates from the 15th century.

Thrupp: Without the Oxford Canal the tiny village of Thrupp might never have evolved. Developed in the late 18th century this stretch of water provided the villagers with work on the barges in the days when this was an important route in the transportation of coal. Today its industrial background is not forgotten, but now the hordes of narrow boats plying the canal carry weekenders and holidaymakers instead of coal.

Bletchingdon Park: The house is late 18th century and was built by James Lewis in the Palladian style on the site of an earlier house which was fortified for Charles I during the Civil War. In April 1645, after some success at Islip routing Lord Northampton's cavalry, Cromwell arrived at Bletchingdon in hot pursuit of the fugitives. He immediately demanded the surrender of the house and the young Royalist Commander, Colonel Windebank, who was the son of the Secretary of State to Charles I, reluctantly yielded to the enemy under pressure from his wife. He was later court-martialled and executed. The nearby church dates back to the 13th century and was restored in 1878. Inside there are memorials to several local families including the Coghills, one of whom married Christopher Wren.

WALK TWO

Steeple Aston, Rousham and The Heyfords

Introduction: A variety of delights awaits you on this walk through the Cherwell valley. Beginning in the pretty stone-built village of Steeple Aston it is only a short stroll to Rousham where you can visit one of Oxfordshire's lesser known splendours — Rousham House and its magnificent gardens designed by William Kent, running down to the banks of the Cherwell. The garden is a horticulturalist's dream.

Beyond Rousham the walk follows the Oxford Canal where it flows alongside the Cherwell between the villages of Lower and Upper Heyford and then swings west to spring one final surprise — a curious hill-top folly just outside Steeple Aston.

Distance: The walk is about 4½ miles long and should take just over 2 hours. Allow longer if you intend visiting Rousham.

Refreshments: The White Lion at Steeple Aston and The Bell Inn at Lower Heyford serve snacks and both have beer gardens. The Three Horseshoes at Upper Heyford provides bar food.

How to get there: North of Oxford take the A423 Banbury road and then, just beyond Hopcraft's Holt and the junction with the B4030, turn right signposted Steeple Aston and follow the road into the village. Park in the vicinity of Heyford Road in the centre.

The Walk: Walk away from the village centre in Steeple Aston (HN) along Heyford Road with The White Lion on your left and the post office and stores over to the right. Pass Jubilee Close on the left and continue ahead. After a minute or two

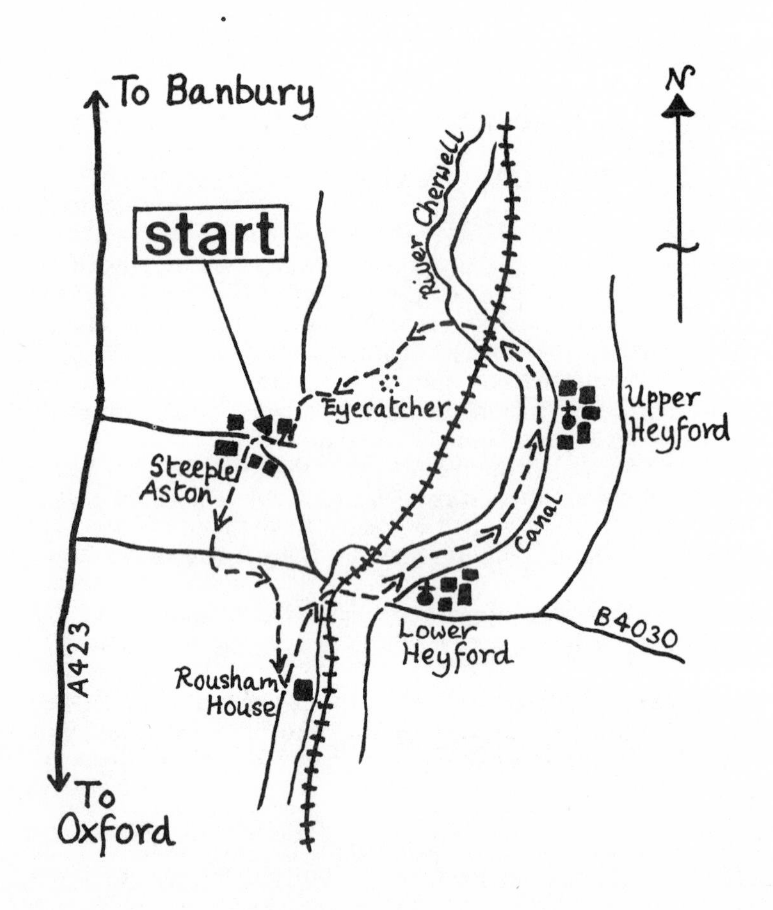
To Banbury
N
start
River Cherwell
Eyecatcher
Upper
Heyford
Steeple
Aston
Canal
B4030
Lower
Heyford
A423
Rousham
House
To
Oxford

you will see on the left a public footpath signpost to Rousham — 1 ¼ miles.

Climb up the bank and follow the path along the left boundary of the field, the church tower at Steeple Aston visible behind you, standing amidst the houses and cottages of the village. Further up the field swing over to the left a little to join a track running along its edge. Follow the track as it heads south cutting between fields and providing good views over rural north Oxfordshire. The buildings of Upper Heyford airfield can be glimpsed over to your extreme left here.

The track narrows to a path and then descends towards a belt of woodland. Pass through a gateway with an adjoining stile and then drop down a steep bank of grass and scrub to another stile with an arrow. Cross the stile, descend the field slope with the woodland on your left and at the bottom go slightly left towards a gap in the bushes and then follow the path to a gate and stile in the left-hand corner of the field.

Cross out into the road, ½ mile into the walk by now, and bear left for several yards and then right, and up a steep bank on the opposite side of the road under a thick canopy of trees. At the top of the bank swing left onto a clear, level path between trees and undergrowth. Apart from the sound of traffic on the road down below this is a delightful wooded stretch of the walk to shade you from the sun on warm summer days.

In a while the path curves round to the right to reach a wooden gate. Go through it and then swing left into the field. From here the parkland boundary wall of Rousham House is just visible beyond the far fence and hedge. Head diagonally right towards the distant field corner. Pass through a line of trees and out across the field towards the road running alongside the parkland boundary. As you cross the field there is a splendid glimpse of Rousham House but watch carefully for it or you may miss it.

In the right corner of the field pass through a gate and out into the road. In order to visit Rousham House and the village turn right and then after several steps bear left signposted Rousham. Progress along the tree-lined drive and soon the houses and cottages of the little manorial village can be seen over to the right. Further on the road forks: left is Rousham House (HN), right is the village and the church located in a charming, peaceful setting a few yards from the main house. As you enter the churchyard there is a poignant reminder of the worthlessness and futility of the First World War for on the right are the graves of two young men, members of the Cottrell-Dormer family who still own Rousham House. Rousham has another distinction: it won the Best Kept Village Award for Oxfordshire in 1972.

Leave the church and retrace your steps along the drive to the road and then turn right. Keep the boundary wall on the right and walk to the traffic lights at the junction. Bear right over the road bridge crossing the Cherwell at a pretty stretch. Once over the bridge look to your right for a splendid view of Rousham House across the fields on the horizon.

Cross the road to a stretch of pavement and after a few moments you pass the entrance to Heyford railway station on the left. Ignore the turning and continue up the road and over the bridge. Below you now the railway and the Oxford Canal run side by side. The village of Lower Heyford (HN) is just along the road in front of you.

After visiting Lower Heyford, return to the village side of the bridge and take the tarmac path to the right of the pavement. Cross the bridge and drop down to the towpath. With the station on your left and the boat yard over to the right, proceed along the path beside the Oxford Canal.

This is a picturesque spot, the canal often busy with brightly painted narrow boats. Although there is activity the pace is still gentle, not taxing, the pleasure seekers of the waterways finding this soothing, unhurried form of recreation irresistible.

Quickly you leave the bustle of the station and the boat yard and soon the canal is lined by trees overhanging this stretch of water. Over to the right there are good views of the church at Lower Heyford and on the left glimpses of the Cherwell running alongside the canal.

Pass a lift bridge with a lane leading into Lower Heyford over on the opposite bank and continue between trees and open fields with the occasional moored narrow boat peeping into view. An unexpected British Waterways sign comes into view further on proclaiming 'Sudden Aircraft Noise — overnight mooring not recommended for the next 1 mile'. This is a reference to planes at nearby Heyford.

Soon there is a delightful view of Upper Heyford (HN) with its church tower, 15th century Perpendicular tithe barn built and buttressed by William of Wykeham, and an old stone manor house over on the right bank. Beyond it there are further glimpses of the village with the gardens of some houses running down to the water's edge. On reaching a lock a little further on you will see a bridge and a lane leading back to the village. Press on along the towpath still with glimpses of fields between the trees. A short distance from the lock you reach another bridge. Here scramble up the bank away from the towpath and go left, crossing a bridge over the Cherwell. Bear right for a few yards and then swing away from the riverbank across the field along a clear path.

Cross another branch of the river and then turn right along the left bank. Behind you there are good glimpses of Upper Heyford and its church tower on the far side of the water. Aim for the railway line up ahead. Here the sound of speeding Inter City trains between Paddington, Oxford, the Midlands and the North often shatters the calm of the countryside.

Pass through the tunnel under the railway and then proceed ahead across the fields with the river on your right. Keep the distant woodland in your sights and look out for a wooden footbridge with an iron railing over to your left. Head towards the bridge and cross it over the brook. Follow the path on the far side running between trees and scrub and then climb up the bank and into the field beside a white painted post with an arrow. If the field is ploughed then cross it by keeping to the left-hand edge. On the far side look out for another white post and a gap in the hedge. Aim for the gap and pass through a gate with an arrow pointing obliquely right. Follow the field edge with woodland and fence on the right and over on the left, in the middle of the field, is the curious spectacle of the Rousham Eyecatcher (HN).

Again, further up the field, there are good views of Upper Heyford on the other side of the valley. In front of you can be seen the houses of Steeple Aston as you approach the end of the walk. Continue down the slope passing another white painted post and an arrow in the right boundary. A little further on join a track and bear right. After a few yards swing right and cross over the stile into a paddock. Keep to the right-hand boundary and in the top right corner go over a stile and then walk up Cow Lane between some pretty stone cottages.

At the junction look across to the right and Steeple Aston church is visible just a few yards away. Turn left into Paines Hill and return to the centre of the village where the walk began.

Historical Notes

Steeple Aston: A village much frequented by the French highwayman, Claude Duval. His activities here eventually brought about his downfall, however, and he was later executed at Tyburn. The nearby inn, Hopcraft's Holt is reputedly haunted by the sound of horses' hooves as Duval rides by. The church of St Peter and St Paul is Early English.

Rousham House: The scenic Cherwell valley with the river flowing peacefully through the gardens is a perfect setting for this splendid Jacobean mansion. Built by Sir Robert Dormer in 1635 on an 'H' plan with mullioned windows, the house was extensively remodelled by William Kent just over 100 years later with a hint of free Gothic style about it. Kent was a coach painter's apprentice who later became an architect and landscape gardener and was responsible for designing the Horse Guards in London in 1745. The beautiful garden at Rousham is a lasting monument to the work of Kent, representing the finest example of English Landscape design.

There is more than a hint of the Italianate about the garden with its cascades and ponds, its groves, the Temple of Echo and the seven-arched portico known as Praeneste. A peaceful stroll along the tree-shaded Long Walk is a must for visitors to Rousham and its sumptuous surroundings.

The gardens are open daily from 10.00 am to 4.30 pm. The House is open on Wednesdays, Sundays and Bank Holidays 2.00 pm to 4.30 pm from April until September inclusive. No children under 15 and no dogs.

Lower Heyford: The village used to be called Heyford Purcell in the days when the Purcell family lived here. Originally the

Purcells came from nearby Newton Purcell. Lower Heyford was the setting for one of the main fords across the Cherwell, prior to the construction of a bridge in the 1270s. The church is mostly 14th century.

Upper Heyford: Once known as Heyford Warren its focal point must be the RAF base for the US Air Force 20th Tactical Fighter Wing. The station dates back to the First World War when it was used to instruct pilots. During the Second World War it became a bomber station before the arrival of the USAF in 1951.

The church was rebuilt in the 19th century and has a 15th century tower.

The Rousham Eyecatcher: The work of William Kent, the Eyecatcher is a buttressed three arched sham instantly reminiscent of a castle gateway and visible on the skyline — hence the name. Its solitary position in a hill-top field outside Steeple Aston makes it hard to find for anyone other than those passing this way on foot. But to see it from near or far is a rewarding experience — confirming Kent's undisputed creative genius.

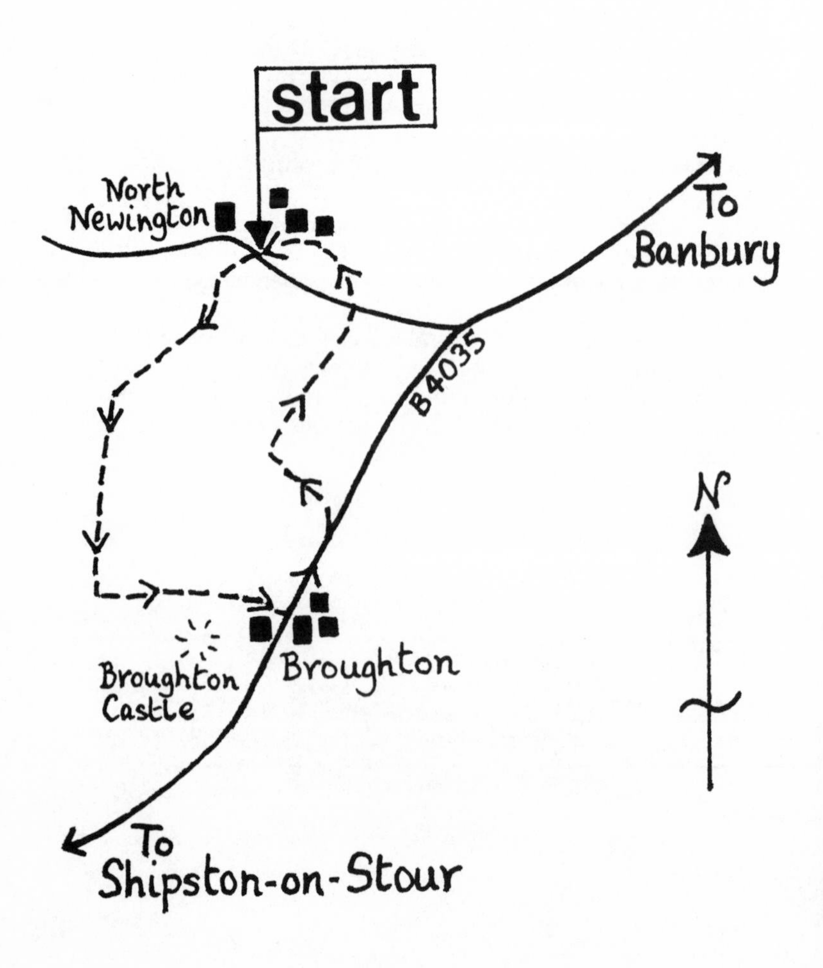
start
North Newington
To Banbury
B4035
N
Broughton Castle
Broughton
To Shipston-on-Stour

WALK THREE

North Newington and Broughton Castle

Introduction: The stroll from North Newington across rolling North Oxfordshire farmland is pleasant and invigorating but surely cannot compare with the splendour of Broughton Castle and its moated site halfway round the walk. Here at the 14th century castle, long associated with the Lords Saye and Sele, and in the surrounding parkland there is an opportunity to pause and admire one of the county's greatest treasures.

Distance: The walk is about 3 miles and should take no more than 1½ hours to complete. Allow longer, however, for a visit to Broughton Castle.

Refreshments: The Blinking Owl Inn at North Newington does bar food. The Saye and Sele Arms in the village of Broughton provides grills and bar snacks and has a garden.

How to get there: From Banbury take the B4035 road and after about 2 miles turn right signposted North Newington. Park in Main Street in the vicinity of the Blinking Owl Inn.

The Walk: From the Blinking Owl Inn in North Newington walk in a westerly direction along Main Street, keeping the inn on the left. Bear left after a few yards onto a stony track known as The Pound. Follow it round to the left and then look for a footpath sign and an arrow on the right in the field boundary

Go into the field and proceed ahead keeping the boundary on the left. At the top of the slope there are grand views over sprawling North Oxfordshire countryside — an undulating carpet of fields and woodland. Behind you in the dip are the houses and cottages of North Newington. Follow the path round to the right as you approach the fence and then head for the far corner of the field close to which is a break in the hedgerow. On reaching the gap go forward onto a grassy track on the edge of the next field and then turn left.

Pass into the next field through another gap in the hedge and then head diagonally right up the sloping field towards a further gap in the distant hedgerow. This is a ploughed field and if difficult to negotiate then follow the boundary instead in order to reach the exit. The higher ground here again provides an excellent viewpoint for a sizeable area of the surrounding countryside.

On reaching the stile cross over it and then bear left following the arrow and keeping the fence on the left. There are good views too over an unspoilt rural landscape to the south.

Proceed to the field corner and then pass through a wooden gate into the next field and continue ahead following the left-hand field boundary down to the road. On reaching the road turn left for several yards and then bear right through a gateway following the direction of the arrow. Keep to the track as far as the hay and straw barns and then swing left onto a path running along a field boundary. A gate and a stile are visible up ahead to the left of some woodland. Cross the stile and continue ahead through the parkland of Broughton Castle (HN). The spire of St Mary's church in Broughton (HN) soon comes into view as does Broughton Castle and its splendid moat over to the right of it.

Continue to the driveway and here you have a choice. If Broughton Castle is open and you intend to visit it turn right and follow the drive round to the left. The church is facing you and if the door is locked the key is available from the addresses listed in the porch. The main entrance to the castle is next to the church.

If you are not visiting Broughton Castle or the church, bear left away from it towards the lodge and on reaching the road turn right. Follow the road into the village of Broughton. When you reach the T junction the Saye and Sele Arms is on your immediate right. On leaving the pub turn left and pass through the village on the B4035 road heading in the direction of Banbury. There is a pavement along this stretch.

Proceed beyond some stone cottages on the right with fields on the left. Pass Danvers Road on the right and just beyond Danvers Barn on the left there is a wooden footpath sign on the left pointing across the fields. Cross the stile and go forward to a double stile in the next field boundary. On reaching the boundary pass into the next field and continue ahead making for a line of trees. At the next stile cross it and proceed over a wooden footbridge across a brook and then cross another stile into the next field.

Cut across the field by heading towards a cottage on the far side. Pass to the left of the cottage and in the field corner adjacent to the garden of the property go through a gate and out into the road. Turn right and follow it as it cuts between fields and hedgerows. The road drops down after a while and then as it begins to rise again turn left after a footpath sign on the right and pass through an open gateway with an adjoining stile. Follow a rough path as far as the stile in the field boundary. Cross over it out into the road. Bear left for a few yards, then swing right signposted Broughton Farm. Pass over a cattle grid and leave the drive by heading to the left across the field, down the dip and up the other side. On reaching the top of the slope go to the right of the stone wall and make for the stile. Cross it and proceed along a grassy path with a house and garden on the right. On reaching Park Lane by the post office in North Newington bear left and walk between stone cottages back to the village centre where the walk began.

Historical Notes

Broughton Castle was built as a fortified manor house by Sir John de Broughton early in the 14th century. Later it passed to William de Wykeham, famous founding father of Winchester School and New College, Oxford. Ninety-nine years after it was built Wykeham set about converting the manor house into a castle, designing battlements and a gatehouse among other additions. In the 15th century Broughton passed by marriage to the Fiennes (pronounced Fines) family when the granddaughter of Sir Thomas Wykeham, great nephew and heir of William, married William Fiennes 2nd Lord Saye and Sele. During the Elizabethan era the house was transformed virtually beyond recognition into the Tudor building you see today. At the time of the Civil War the Fiennes were staunch supporters of the Parliamentarians and did much to defend this corner of the county. One of Broughton's greatest attributes is the 14th century private chapel approached by a stone staircase from the groined passage.

Broughton is still the ancestral home of the Lords Saye and Sele and is open from May to September, Wednesdays and Sundays; also Thursdays in July and August; Bank Holiday Sundays and Mondays including Easter; 2 pm to 5 pm.

The parish church of St Mary is mostly 14th century and has an imposing tower crowned by a fine spire. Inside there are monuments and tombs to all the notable figures connected with Broughton Castle including a painted tomb of Sir John de Broughton.

WALK FOUR

Chipping Norton and The Rollright Stones

Introduction: This walk in the north-west corner of Oxfordshire seems to assume a totally separate identity from those rambles to be found elsewhere in the county. It is different, more redolent of the north of England with its rolling hills, stone houses and walls. The walk begins in Chipping Norton the highest town in Oxfordshire and 'gateway to the Cotswolds'.

Beyond the delightful villages of Salford and Little Rollright the route reaches the Rollright Stones which comprise the Whispering Knights, the King's Men and the King Stone. These intriguing stones are associated with a charming legend. It seems a king was leading his army hereabouts while five of his knights stood together conspiring against him. The King met a witch nearby who told him he would be King of England if he could see the village of Long Compton in seven long strides. As he approached the top of the ridge a mound of earth suddenly rose up before him preventing him from seeing the village and so the king, his soldiers and his knights were all turned to stone.

Many visitors to the Rollright Stones have questioned their origin over the years but they remain a mystery. Appropriate for such a legend as this the remote hilltop setting of these stones has more than a hint of the supernatural about it.

Distance: The walk is about 5½ miles and should take 2¾ to 3 hours. Allow longer for a visit to the Rollright Stones.

Refreshments: There are inns and hotels in Chipping Norton. The Black Horse at Salford offers bar food.

How to get there: From the A34 Oxford to Stratford-on-Avon

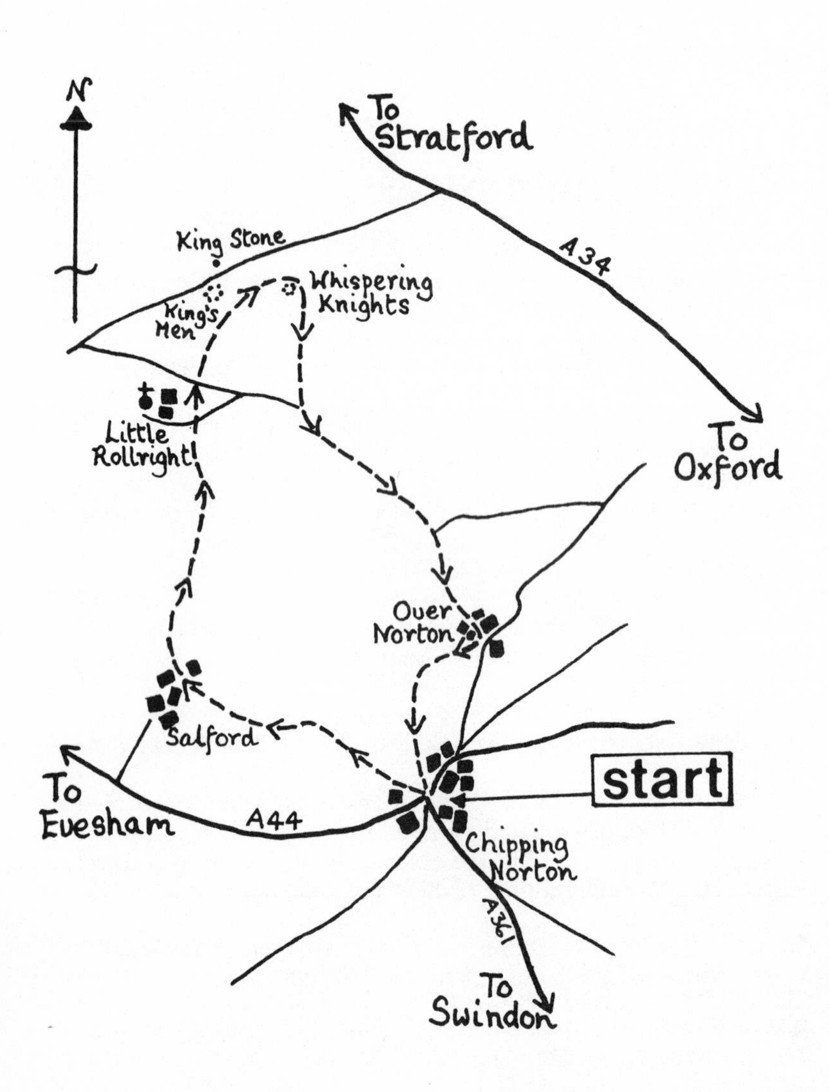
N
To
Stratford
A34
King Stone
Whispering
Knights
King's
Men
Little
Rollright
To
Oxford
Over
Norton
Salford
start
To
Evesham
A44
Chipping
Norton
A361
To
Swindon

road turn left onto the A44 for Chipping Norton. There is plenty of room to park in the town centre.

The Walk: From the town centre in Chipping Norton (HN) turn into New Street and follow the A44 as it descends the hill. Just past Penhurst School and a private road on the right go through a wrought iron kissing gate, the entrance to a recreation ground. Follow the left hand boundary, keeping quite close to a line of trees and aim towards a post and a kissing gate to the left of an adventure playground. Over to the left, between the trees, you may catch a glimpse of Chipping Norton's famous Victorian Bliss Valley Tweed Mill on the outskirts of the town.

Go through the kissing gate and down across the field towards a bridge in the dip. Cross a small stream and then as you head up the hill the path forks. Take the right hand branch and head up towards some houses at the top. Aim to the left of them and look out for a stile in the near boundary. Cross the stile, go over a tarmac drive and then negotiate a second stile leading into the next field. Proceed to the top of the field and in the right hand corner cross over another stile.

Progress by following the right hand edge of the field with a hedgerow and a line of trees on your immediate right. In the corner swing left, then after a few yards turn right through a gap in the hedge and follow the right hand edge of the next field. The views from this stretch of the path are particularly spectacular: a landscape characterised by soft rolling hills and distant villages. This is the north-west corner of Oxfordshire, only a mile or two from where this glorious county meets Warwickshire to the north and the distinctive beauty of one of Britain's most popular regions — the Cotswolds — to the west.

Follow the track down through the field; ignore a left hand path and continue to where it swings sharp right. Here, bear left through the gateway into a field and proceed in much the same direction by following the left boundary. A large copse is clearly visible a little to the right now and over to the east you may catch a brief glimpse of an old disused railway tunnel. Keep to the field edge and in the corner join a cart track running along the boundary of the next field. As you walk along the track look for lines of poplar trees on the slopes of the far hillside. Just before the cart track curves right in the field corner join a parallel path on the left and follow it between trees and hedgerows towards the village of Salford. Go through a gate and up to the village green. To visit the Black Horse continue ahead past the green and a telephone box. The road curves right and then left and the Inn is on the corner.

On leaving the Black Horse return to the green and take the turning marked Trout Lakes-Rectory Farm. Pass a footpath sign on the left to Little Rollright and continue ahead between the poplar trees. Soon there is a turning on the right to Lower Lake. Ignore this and press on between the fields, following a sign to Top Lake. When the track swings sharp right, go straight on keeping to a waymarked path along the right hand edge of the field. Proceed to the field corner, pass through a gap and then along the left hand boundary of the next field. In a minute or two swing diagonally left across the field, following the direction of the arrow and making for the top left-hand corner. On reaching it glance back for a splendid view out over the Oxfordshire countryside, the landscape a network of fields and hedgerows. A trout lake is just visible down below among the trees. Cross the stile and descend the slope towards Little Rollright. The church can be seen on the lower slopes of the far hillside, its delightful setting hardly changed by the passing centuries.

At the bottom go through a gap and onto a track running between corrugated barns. Follow the track to the road and then bear left along it in order to visit Little Rollright (HN) and St Philip's church.

From the church turn left and head back down the lane. Follow it round to the right and then left and after a few yards bear left onto a signposted footpath. Pass some old buildings including stables and press on up the grassy incline. On reaching a field go slightly left, following the direction of the arrow, towards a post in the far boundary. Cross out into the road and then go through a white gate opposite and onto a track running along the right hand edge of the field.

When the track peters out continue ahead along the field boundary. Pass into the next field and proceed ahead towards a line of trees. A backward glance here reveals a glorious view: a rolling patchwork of fields and trees and hedgerows with the village of Over Norton and neighbouring Chipping Norton on the distant skyline.

On reaching the field boundary it is worth deviating from the route for a few minutes in order to visit the Rollright Stones. Bear left and after a minute or two you come upon The Whispering Knights (HN), a set of five stones enclosed by iron railings. Continue along the edge of the field, out into the road and then turn left. Follow the road for a short distance (300-400 yards) and the entrance to The King's Men (HN), a stone circle, is on the left. After visiting the site return to the road which incidentally forms the county boundary between Oxfordshire and Warwickshire. On the opposite side, just into Warwickshire, is the entrance to The King Stone (HN). The monument commands a splendid position high above the rolling hills and valleys with the charming old village of Long Compton nestling just below you.

Return to the Whispering Knights and continue ahead along the field edge. Cross over the footpath from Little Rollright and with a belt of woodland on your left follow the field boundary down as far as the corner. Pass through a gap in the hedge and head diagonally right towards an opening in the far corner. On reaching the gap, go obliquely left across the next field to the footpath sign in the boundary and then out into the road.

Bear left and after some time pass the old railway embankment. Begin climbing the hill and in a while turn right, signposted Over Norton. Pass some allotments; on the right there are good views across the hills towards Chipping Norton and over to Salford in the west.

Drop down into Over Norton and at the junction turn right. When the road swings left with Cleeves Corner on the right go forward onto a grit drive. Pass the entrance to a house, High Cleeves, on the left. Beyond it there are glimpses of Chipping Norton through the trees. Follow the path over this high ground and soon an old corrugated hangar comes into view on the right. Pass the entrance to it, continue along the track and, immediately before the hedge gives way to open boundaries on the left, turn left into a field and walk down its right hand boundary with the hedge on the right. Descend the slope heading towards the buildings of Chipping Norton, the church clearly seen on the other hillside. Pass into the next field through the gap and continue almost to the bottom and then turn right towards a primitive section of fencing concealed among the trees.

Cross over onto a clear path running down through the field towards a belt of trees at the bottom. Aim for the kissing gate in the left corner of the field, go through it and onto a path running up the hill. Follow the path with a stone wall on the right; a substantial stone-built house soon comes into view beyond the wall. Proceed between wall and fence and a little further the parish church can be seen through the trees immediately on the right.

At the top of the rise pass a cottage on the left and a path shooting off to the right. Follow the track round to the right between stone walls and cottages. Turn right at the junction and head back to Chipping Norton where the walk began.

Historical Notes

Little Rollright: The manor house was once important. It was the home of William Blower who gave St Philip's church its pinnacled tower in 1617. The church which is 15th century has two 17th century monuments to the Dixon and Blower families.

The Whispering Knights: Originally a Stone Age tomb covered by a barrow or mound. The Knights — of which there are five — are upright stones, four of them stand huddled together protecting and enclosing a fifth.

The King's Men: These comprise 60 stones arranged in an unditched circle about 100 ft. across and ranging in size from just a few inches to 7ft. Here and there the stones almost touch and at one time may have formed an unbroken wall.

The King Stone: Enclosed by railings, it stands alone and apart from the others, just across the county boundary into Warwickshire. The 8 ft tall monolith stands on a low mound thought to have been a long barrow in which Stone Age chieftains were buried.

WALK FIVE

Charlbury and Wychwood Forest

Introduction: Above all, this is a walk of immense variety and exceptional beauty. Beyond Charlbury and the peaceful village of Chilson the walk quickly enters Wychwood Forest. The 1,301 acre forest, once a Royal hunting ground much favoured by Plantagenet kings, includes some of the loveliest scenery in the whole of Oxfordshire. It is also one of the least visited parts of the county for until 1988 public access was severely restricted — hence its reputation locally as the secret forest. Now ramblers and visitors may stroll among the trees and grassy rides for 1½ miles. However, because of deer culling and pheasant rearing the County Council request that you keep dogs on leads and do not stray from the public rights-of-way.

Emerging from the peace and beauty of the forest at Finstock you soon reach Cornbury Park with its graceful deer and its splendid house glimpsed from the estate lodges. Here, for the second time, the walk crosses the Evenlode river described by Belloc as 'a lovely river, all alone . . . forgotten in the western wolds'.

Distance: The walk is about 8 miles; 3¼ hours should be enough time to complete it.

Refreshments: There are several inns at Charlbury including The Bell which offers light meals at the bar and The Bull which provides home cooked food and has a beer garden. The Crown at Finstock serves bar meals at lunchtime and in the evening.

How to get there: From Oxford follow the A34 Stratford road and about 2 miles beyond Woodstock bear left onto the B4437 Charlbury road. In the town make for the Spendlove Centre which is signposted and use the car park there.

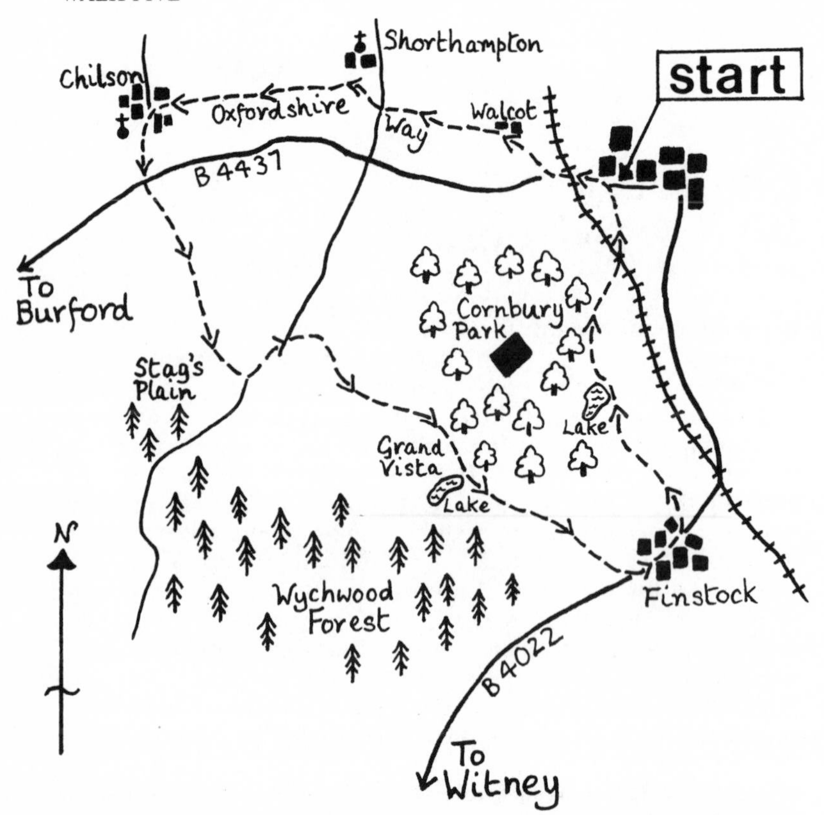

The Walk: Turn right out of the car park at the Spendlove Centre in Charlbury (HN) and walk down to the junction by The Bull. Bear right and pass the post office on the right and then the Quaker Meeting House on the same side. Turn left at The White Hart, signposted Dyers Hill, railway station and Burford. As you descend the hill note the simple station building peeping into view ahead below the wooded slopes of Wychwood Forest.

Cross over the pretty Evenlode, its water plants swirling freely against the river bed and a few yards beyond the bridge on the left is the entrance to Charlbury railway station. Glancing back at this point there is a good view of Charlbury up on the hill, its lines of old houses and cottages clinging to the slopes with the church tower visible a little to the right.

Follow the B4437 road over the railway line and away from the buildings of Charlbury. Begin to ascend the slope and then after about 200 yards swing right onto a bridleway signposted Walcot. This is part of the Oxfordshire Way, a long distance path of over 60 miles stretching from the Cotswolds to the Chilterns and finishing at Henley-on-Thames. Keep on the bridleway and when the drive bears right beyond a pair of cottages to reach Walcot Farm continue ahead along the stony track, still the Oxfordshire Way, towards Chilson.

An old barn with a dilapidated roof comes into view now and over to the right the scene is a delightful mixture of fields and woodland across the Evenlode valley. The trees of Wychwood Forest are clearly visible to the south.

Follow the track as it becomes progressively more grassy underfoot and soon you pass an old beech tree on the left with a white arrow pointing ahead. Beyond the tree the track drops down quite sharply and then quickly rises again the other side. Ultimately you reach a gate; go through it and then turn right for a few yards along the road. At the junction take the left turning signposted Shorthampton and follow the tarmac lane with views on the right over to the village of Chadlington just below the skyline.

When the lane bends right follow it and very soon you are in Shorthampton with the little church of All Saints (HN) on the left. The lane runs through this peaceful hamlet in the shape of a loop. On returning to the church proceed ahead to the bend and continue the walk by turning right.

At the next corner go through a gate and follow the waymarked track as it weaves a somewhat erratic route down through the fields. Descend the slope and then climb up the other side, the track narrowing to a path. The buildings of Chilson are apparent now. At the top of the slope the path widens out again and is bordered by hedges.

Continue ahead onto a grit track and on reaching the road turn left, following the Oxfordshire Way arrow. You are now in the main street of Chilson, a charming village of stone houses and cottages. Proceed along the street, leaving the long distance footpath now as it swings right and heads for Ascott-under-Wychwood a mile or so across the fields to the south-west.

Follow the road away up the hill to the junction. Turning for a moment there is a good view from here back to Chilson, the village sitting snugly against the hills on the far side of the valley. Turn right signposted Burford and then after 100 yards bear left at a sign — 'No Through Road-Chilson Hill only'. Walk up the metalled drive past some cottages on the left and continue ahead on a grassy path.

Follow the path round to the left and then almost immediately turn right before the corner of the hedge. Go towards a waymarker post and on reaching it swing left and then in the field corner bear right and follow the path along the left boundary. In the next corner pass through a gap in the hedge and proceed ahead onto a track, following it along the side of the field with woodland on the left.

Soon the trees give way to a field, albeit briefly, and within moments there is a screen of trees, bracken and scrub on your left. Go through a gateway with an arrow beside it and into the woods. Progress up the hill, avoiding a track on the left and on the right, and continue between trees and bracken.

Follow the path as it curves right; here the route is lined by rows of fir trees. The path swings left and then right after a few yards between bracken clearings. Proceed along the path and soon there are views over open parkland to the left. Further on, still with parkland views, the path curves left and runs under the branches of adjacent beech trees until it joins the road at Stag's Plain.

Turn left and follow the road as it swings to the right. After several bends you pass the entrance to Waterman's Lodge Stables on the left. Immediately past the turning, on the right, is a stile giving access into Wychwood Forest (HN). Cross the stile noting the sign 'Dogs must not be allowed to stray from the footpath', and after several yards join the track and bear right into the forest. Avoid the right hand turning and take the bend. When, after a few yards, the track swings right, proceed ahead following the direction of the arrow. The trees overhang along this stretch forming a protective tunnel.

Pass over a cross-track and continue with clear glimpses of fields over to the left. An old beech tree comes into view a little further on, its ancient trunk gnarled and weathered by the years. Descend through the forest following a broad grassy ride lined by trees and clearings. Further on you will see a white gate over on the left. Swing right here across one of the approaches to Cornbury Park known as the Grand Vista, and join a track running between trees and banks of scrub.

Pass some old barns on the left and continue ahead as the track descends steeply between the trees. There is a lake at the bottom on the right. Turn left as you draw level with it and follow the track up the hill bearing left when you reach the fork at the top. Shortly, as the track veers left proceed ahead onto a narrow path between bracken and undergrowth and, after a few yards, cross a stile.

Now you are on a pretty stretch of path on the edge of the forest with good views of fields and woodland over to your right. Almost at once you pass a turning on the left with a 'Private Footpath' sign. Continue ahead along the grassy path and further up the slope it cuts between ploughed fields with the houses of Finstock slowly becoming visible over on the skyline. At length the path graduates to a drive before reaching the B4022 road on the outskirts of Finstock (HN). Bear left at the junction and walk down the road. In a while you reach a turning on the right to North Leigh and Wilcote and here, just beyond the war memorial, you will spot The Crown public house.

Continue along the B4022 towards Charlbury; pass some obsolete farm buildings on the left and follow the road between lines of trees. When the road curves right bear left onto a waymarked tarmac drive. Finstock railway station is a little further on along the main road.

Follow the drive down between the fields, curving firstly right and then left. There are good views to the right across the Evenlode valley with the route of the Oxfordshire Way on the distant horizon as it travels in a south-easterly direction out of Charlbury.

Pass some barns on the left and now the drive is straight, running between trees and paddocks. Go through a gateway with a sign 'Drive slow — Horses. Thank you'. Proceed over a ramp and continue along the drive with pleasant vistas through an avenue of oak trees. You are now on the edge of Cornbury Park (HN).

Beyond some cottages on the right you reach a stud with its

gathering of Cotswold stone buildings and then, on the left of the drive, a lake with an inscription in the wall beside the path:-

'Cream of Lanfine
Born April 10th, 1970
Died 24th May, 1977
Avon's best friend'

The plaque is in memory of a dog belonging to the son of Lord Rotherwick of Cornbury Park.

Pass South Hill Cottage and then go through a white gate with a footpath sign to the right of a cattle grid. Follow the grassy path with a wrought iron fence on your immediate left and woodland on your right. Beyond the fence is Cornbury deer park where you can easily spot the graceful movements of the deer herd as they break cover from the trees.

Further on the trees on the left of the fence bend down their branches to overhang the path. Pass another huge tree trunk and then cross a stile. Proceed to the next stile and then on over several more. There are glimpses of Charlbury over to the right now on the far hillside.

Descend the slope and then head up the incline to another stile located between some trees. Once over it go forward to a wooden gate with a footpath sign attached to it to the left of some garages. Go through the gate and on your left now are the impressive twin estate lodges guarding the magnificent entrance to Cornbury Park. Proceed to the drive and as you join it look left through the imposing gates and down the avenue of trees to the main house beyond.

Turn right and walk away from the entrance, over the Evenlode once again, the river rushing headlong down below you between the trees. Cross the railway line and, on reaching the road, turn left and head back to the Spendlove Centre in Charlbury where the walk began.

Historical Notes

Charlbury: It has grown over the years but the centre of this popular town, now a conservation area, still retains its old-fashioned charm. Once Charlbury was a market town following the clearing of the forests for farming. A few interesting old buildings remain including the 18th century Friends' meeting house and the 19th century Methodist and Baptist chapels. The church of St Mary the Virgin is Norman and was enlarged in the 13th century and restored in the 1870s. The railway station is a listed building.

The Church of All Saints, Shorthampton: The tiny Norman church includes a three decker 18th century pulpit, box pews and some interesting medieval wall paintings which were discovered under many coats of limewash whilst restoration work was being carried out.

Wychwood Forest: Over 600 acres of the forest have been designated a National Nature Reserve by the Nature Conservancy Council and include many different species of trees and wild plants. Until the late 1980s ramblers had only been allowed access to the forest, part of Lord Rotherwick's Cornbury Park Estate, one day a year, on Palm Sunday. For this reason it came to be known locally as the 'secret forest'. However, a 24 year battle between Lord Rotherwick and the Ramblers' Association ended in victory when the Environment Department granted an application by the county council for the path following a public inquiry.

Finstock: Together with its neighbour Fawler, Finstock was originally built by the Romans. The church is mid 19th century and constructed of local stone. Two stained glass windows commemorate Queen Victoria's Jubilee in 1887. The churchyard contains the grave of Jane, Baroness Churchill who died in 1900, just before Queen Victoria, to whom she was maid and confidante for over 40 years.

Cornbury Park: Home of Lord Rotherwick, the park includes a part of Wychwood Forest. The Tudor 17th and 18th century mansion was once the largest in Oxfordshire before Blenheim Palace. Cornbury was the home of Robert Dudley, Elizabeth I's Earl of Leicester, and where Lord Clarendon, companion to the two Charles Stuarts, also resided. His daughter married James II.

WALK SIX

Farmoor Reservoir, Bablock Hythe and The Thames

Introduction: Water is very much the theme of this walk. Beginning on the banks of Farmoor Reservoir the path heads south, keeping close to the water's edge but not always within sight of it. Sailing is a regular activity here as is fishing and bird-watching; such is the popularity and scope that this huge expanse of water gives the impression of being a natural lake rather than a reservoir supplying the Oxford area.

Further on the path reaches Bablock Hythe, known locally for its associations with the poet Matthew Arnold and where a ferry used to cross the Thames. The final leg is a delightful stroll beside the river as it meanders in a series of sweeping curves and bends through the flat countryside. The walk returns to the banks of the reservoir just as the Thames reaches pretty Pinkhill Lock.

Distance: Just under 3 hours should be enough time to allow for this walk. The route is approximately 5½ miles.

Refreshments; There are no public houses on the walk but The Bear and Ragged Staff at nearby Cumnor provides bar food. Elsewhere there are plenty of places ideal for a picnic.

How to get there: From the A34 near Oxford take the A420 road signposted Swindon and Bristol. Turn off for Cumnor after about 2 miles and then leave the village by following the signs for Farmoor. Follow the road for about 1½ miles and then, on reaching Farmoor Reservoir, turn left through Gate 3 and into the car park.

The Walk: Leave the car park by joining the path at the southern end, marked 'Farmoor Countryside Walk'. Follow the

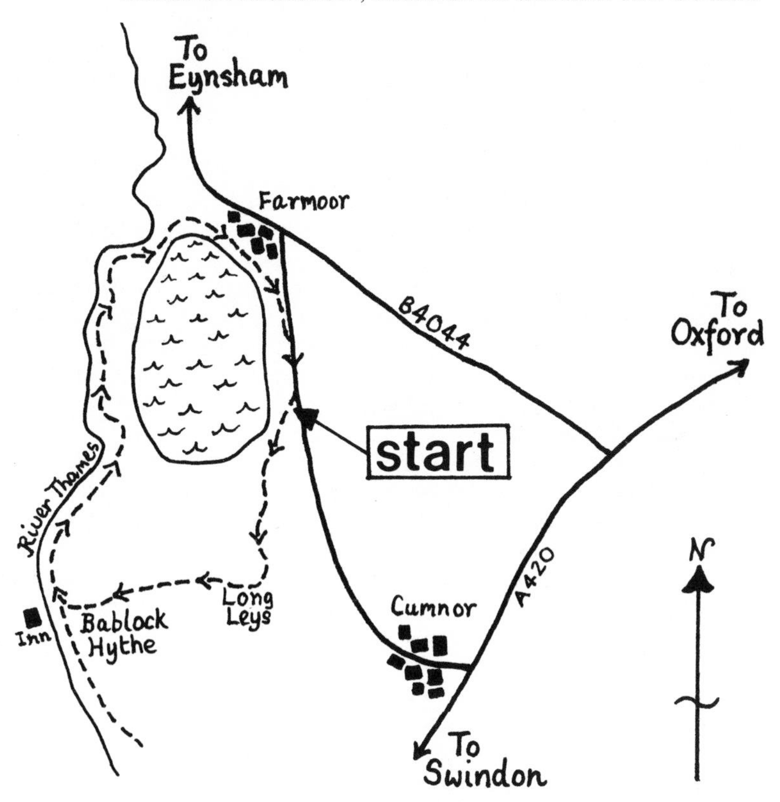

path as it twists and turns and at the toilet block go over the stile and continue ahead along the right-hand edge of the field. After a short distance pause for a spectacular view right across Farmoor Reservoir. Glancing back the houses of Farmoor village are visible from here, beneath the slopes of Wytham Woods.

Continue into the next field; keep to the right-hand edge and a little further on cross a stile leading onto a grassy path. After a few yards the path, signposted with arrows, turns left to reach another stile. Cross over it and then head for the stile on the opposite side of the drive.

Follow the right-hand edge of the field heading in the direction of the wooded slopes. On reaching the footpath sign at the end of the fence on the right, go slightly right across the field passing through a line of electricity pylons and making towards a farm up on the hill. Pass through the gap in the hedge, over a wooden footbridge followed by a stile and then go straight ahead to the stile in the next fence.

Cross the stile and turn right heading up the field towards the farm buildings. Pass through the gate in the right-hand corner of the field and continue ahead keeping to the right of the buildings. Immediately beyond them bear left to cross over a track after a few yards. Continue in the same direction and aim for the tennis court in front of you. Turn left just before it to join a drive. Continue ahead with the tennis court on the right and the attractive stone farmhouse on the left. Stay on the drive until you reach the main junction.

For a visit to Cumnor turn left and follow the lane for several minutes. On reaching a thatched cottage on the right turn right and follow the track into the trees. When the track swings left to form the entrance to a house proceed ahead on a narrow path into the field. Follow the path along the left boundary of the field, cross the stile and continue ahead through the next field to another stile. Once over the stile turn right along a path and after about 50 yards emerge at the road in Cumnor beside a pond. The Bear & Ragged Staff is a short distance to your right.

To resume the walk return by the same route to the entrance to the farm and continue ahead. Pass through a gate almost immediately and head down the track known as the Long Leys with the pylons visible in the distance. There are brief glimpses of Farmoor Reservoir over to the right beyond the trees. A short distance before the pylons, join a rough cart track and continue.

In a while the track swings left between trees and bushes. This stretch can be particularly wet and muddy in places after a spell of rain. The track meanders for some time, at length narrowing to a path cutting between trees and sometimes thick undergrowth. Finally, it emerges onto a track. Follow the track ahead and at the junction bear right and after a few yards you reach the riverbank of the Thames at Bablock Hythe (HN).

Make for the stile at the far end of the parking area and after crossing it proceed across the field keeping to the left-hand edge with the Thames on your immediate left. Follow the field edge as the river begins to sweep round to the right with lines of caravans on the opposite bank and motor cruisers moored down at the water's edge. Continue beside the Thames with good views of the wooded slopes around Wytham Hill on the horizon. Head towards a gate in the field corner. Go through it and walk along a grassy path with a fence on the right and the river on the left. Pass over a stream, through another gate and continue ahead with the river still on your left.

Keep to the water's edge as the river swings left, pass through a gate and continue. Though the vast expanse of water that is Farmoor Reservoir is not visible on this stretch of the walk, the long low bank on the right signifies its western boundary. The river bears round to the right again; go through another gate and keep to the riverbank. In a while the path swings sharp right and passes through two gates with a wooden footbridge in between, shaded by the trees of a little copse. Emerge from the trees after a few yards and continue parallel with the river.

Pass a public footpath sign and head towards the Thames Water Authority building up ahead. On reaching it ignore a stile on the right and proceed ahead over a stile and along the riverbank. Cross the concrete bridge, pass the 'source works' sign and continue beside the river.

Soon the Thames swings sharp right and then bears left by some trees. Cross the stile here but now, instead of keeping to the riverbank, follow the fence on your immediate right and when you reach a kissing gate pass through it and up onto a metalled drive circling the reservoir. Turn left and follow the drive with good views to the left over to Pinkhill Lock. Ignore a turning on the left leading down to the lock and continue to the next gate. Pass through an adjacent kissing gate and follow a path which turns right by a stile. Keep on the path bordered by wire fencing as it runs parallel with the drive. Shortly the path swings left, crossing a bridge over a stream.

Once over the bridge turn immediately right onto a grassy path running between hedges and banks of undergrowth with the houses of Farmoor visible on the left. Continue along the path following a line of pylons and at length the borders of greenery give way to an extended clearing. Continue ahead and soon a gate comes into view up ahead slightly to your left. Pass through the gate and out into the road.

Immediately on your right is Farmoor Source Works, opened in 1967 as denoted on the plaque at the main gate. Proceed ahead along the grass verge, passing Gate 2 and very quickly reaching Gate 3. Turn right here and back into the car park where the walk began.

Historical Notes

Bablock Hythe: Matthew Arnold, the 19th century poet, knew this place well. His local walks included Bablock Hythe and the surrounding countryside and he made references to these much loved haunts in his *Scholar Gipsy*.

> 'Thee, at the ferry Oxford riders blithe,
> Returning home on summer nights, have met
> Crossing the stripling Thames at Bablock-hithe,
> Trailing in the cool stream thy fingers wet,
> As the punt's rope chops round.'

There was indeed once a ferry across the Thames at this point but now the lane runs out at the water's edge accommodating the likes of picnickers, fishermen and local residents. The Ferryboat Inn at Bablock Hythe was where young Betty Rudge was employed as a maidservant in the 1760s. And thereby hangs a charming but ultimately tragic tale of 18th century romance. Betty's father was a nearby weirkeeper and after her work at the inn she would walk home along the riverbank to her father's cottage. One day she encountered a young Oxford undergraduate along the riverbank and they fell into conversation. He was quickly enchanted by her natural beauty and unspoilt nature and soon love blossomed between them. What gives the story added interest is the fact that her suitor was William Flower, Viscount Ashbrook a member of the nobility and she was only a humble maidservant. However, in spite of their different backgrounds theirs seemed a perfect match and they were married in 1766, setting up home together above Bablock Hythe before moving to nearby Shellingford. But Betty's happiness was short-lived. She lost two children in infancy and sadly the Viscount himself died in 1780 at the age of 37.

WALK SEVEN

Badbury Hill and Great Coxwell

Introduction: Badbury Hill, a mile or so to the west of Faringdon, is an ideal point from which to begin a walk through some of Oxfordshire's loveliest countryside. Overlooking the Vale of the White Horse the hill is a splendid amenity area. There is room for picnicking and many visitors come here simply for a quiet stroll in the shade of the trees.

Half way round the walk is the village of Coleshill with its pretty cottages and handsome church tower overlooking the green. Two miles further on is another village — Great Coxwell — boasting a magnificent old medieval tithe barn, one of the largest in the country and described by William Morris as being as noble as a cathedral. The Great Barn is now in the care of the National Trust. The church at Great Coxwell, dedicated to St Giles, stands on a knoll above the village and from it there are impressive views over the surrounding fields and pastures.

Distance: The walk is about 5½ miles long and should take 2-2½ hours to complete.

Refreshments: The Radnor Arms at Coleshill provides bar snacks at lunchtime and in the evenings.

How to get there: From Faringdon on the A420 Oxford to Swindon road, head west on the B4019 road signposted Highworth and the entrance to Badbury Hill car park will be found on the right after about 1½ miles.

The Walk: From the car park at Badbury Hill (HN) proceed forward to the gate and stile at the far end and then join the track beyond winding between the trees. Initially the track runs roughly parallel with the B4019 road and over to the

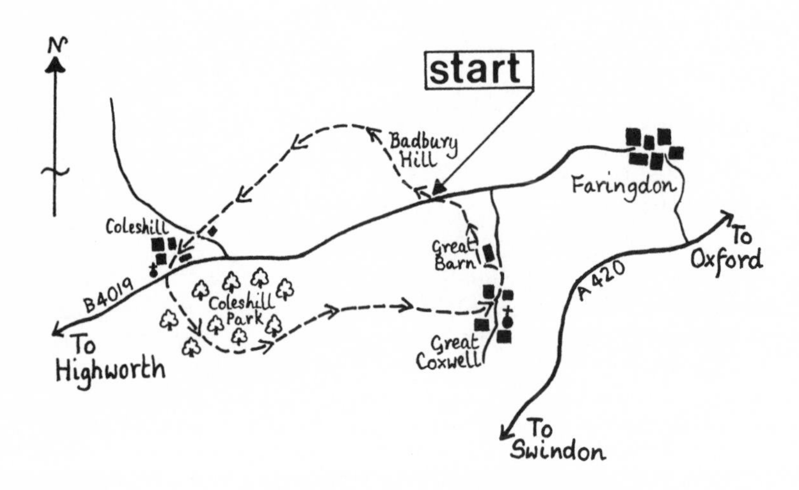

left between the trees there are glimpses of distant downland beyond the Vale of the White Horse.

Shortly you reach a pretty stone cottage on the right set peacefully in the woodland. Pass over a cross-track and continue ahead. After a while the path drops down through the woods somewhat steeply. Cross over a main track and continue down between the trees. Soon the path levels out as you reach the bottom of Badbury Hill, emerging from the trees on the edge of a field. Follow the right-hand boundary of the field heading towards Brimstone Farm. In the field corner go left, cross the bridge over the stream on your right and then continue ahead along the right-hand edge of the next field. After passing the farmhouse on the right the path reaches a track with farm buildings opposite. Cross over and take the track immediately to the left of the buildings. Keep to it for a few yards and then cross the stile in the left-hand fence and go obliquely right across the field, making for the gap in the hedge up ahead. Negotiate the stile, cross the footbridge and then follow the right-hand edge of the field. Bear left at the field corner and then turn right and cross into the next field again by means of a wooden footbridge and a stile.

Follow a clear path enclosed by a hedge and fence and at the next stile continue ahead along the right-hand boundary of the field. Follow it down to the corner by the trees, cross the stile then the stream via the wooden footbridge and keep to the path along the edge of the woodland. Soon you reach another stile. Cross it and emerge from the woodland at a field corner. Proceed ahead up the right-hand edge of the field. There is a short pull up here and at the top it is worth pausing for a backward glance at the wooded slopes of Badbury Hill on the easterly horizon. Looking to the north, beyond the farm, there are splendid views across Oxfordshire.

Continue the walk by following the edge of the fields. Pass a small pond in a hollow surrounded by trees on the right and look for the outline of the 15th century church tower at Coleshill up ahead as you approach the field corner. Pass through the gap and out to the road, cross the stile on the opposite side and, once in the field, go slightly to the right of the trees and fence in front of you. Drop down the slope keeping the wire fence on your left and at the bottom pass through a kissing gate with an adjoining footpath sign and out into the lane.

Continue ahead, making for the church and the village centre in Coleshill (HN). Just beyond the church the lane reaches the village green and the main B4019 road. For refreshment turn left here and walk up the road past the village post office and telephone box on the right to reach the Radnor Arms on the left. Return to the green and turn left along the lane opposite (signposted Gt Coxwell 2½ miles). On reaching the sign for Coleshill Nurseries continue ahead along the waymarked drive immediately to the left of a house. Through the gate the path runs across farmland belonging to Coleshill Park. The path ahead can be seen threading its way across the landscape until it disappears from view in the vast patchwork of fields laid out before you. There are splendid teasing glimpses of distant downland characteristically topped with bursts of trees.

Cross the field to the stile and continue through the next field by keeping straight ahead along the narrow path between the crops. Head towards the gate in the far boundary and, on reaching it, cross two stiles with a ditch in between. Continue ahead to the next stile a short distance away in the next field boundary. Cross it and then proceed up the slope towards a clump of trees. The trunk of the left-hand tree has a white arrow pointing ahead. The White Horse at Uffington is visible from here across the fields.

Press on ahead towards the downland horizon and soon you reach a wide track. Turn left and follow it keeping to the left-hand edge of the field with trees and bushes on the left. Shortly farm buildings come into view ahead. On reaching the farm cross the track and go straight ahead keeping to the left of the buildings. Proceed into the right-hand field and cross it by going diagonally left towards the stile in the far hedge and fence. Cross the stile then a second one and head across the next field making for the stile in the distant hedgerow. The church tower at Great Coxwell peeps into view now.

Negotiate the stile, bear round to the left through the little spinney, pass over the ditch by means of a wooden footbridge and then, after crossing yet another stile, turn right onto a farm track. Immediately the track bears left and then right following the field boundary.

Keep to the left edge of the fields at all times as you approach the houses and cottages of Great Coxwell. At length, after passing through several fields and crossing a stile and footbridge, the path swings right by a corrugated fence in the field corner. A few yards beyond the fence bear left through a gate and head along a narrow path to the road. Turn left and walk along the main village street of Great Coxwell (HN).

Pass a variety of cottages, houses and bungalows. Note St Giles church up on the hill to the right and continue to the outskirts of the village. When you reach the magnificent Great Barn on the left it is worth pausing for a few moments in order to visit the great historic National Trust building and enjoy its fine setting.

From the main door of the Great Barn walk down towards the pond and just to the right of it is a gate with an adjoining stile. Cross the stile into the field and turn right towards the trees, the Great Barn now on your right. Keep to the path as it winds along the right-hand side of the field. Soon you draw level with the trees, then turn right over a stile into the woodland. Cross a stream immediately and then follow the clear path. At the next stile cross over and then directly turn right and walk along a grassy track. Follow the track to the road and then turn left and walk back to the car park at Badbury Hill, the entrance being on the right.

Historical Notes

Badbury Hill rises to 500ft and is crowned with trees. It is the site of an Iron Age hill-fort and is in the care of the National Trust.

Coleshill: Sadly the great 17th century house at Coleshill Park is no more. Destroyed by fire in the mid 1950s, only the park remains. Built between 1650 and 1662 by Roger Pratt the house boasted a splendid staircase generally acknowledged to be the finest of its kind. Originally the manor was in the ownership of William Edington, Bishop of Worcester. Later it passed to the Pleydell family whose daughter married William Bouverie, later Baron Pleydell Bouverie of Coleshill and Earl of Radnor.

St Giles church, Great Coxwell is mostly 13th century and has a Perpendicular top to its 15th century tower. The pulpit is Jacobean and the tracery on the north doorway is certainly worth closer inspection.

The Great Barn: About 150ft long and 50ft wide The Great Barn was completed around the middle of the 13th century by the Cistercian Monks of Beaulieu Abbey to whom King John gave the Manor in 1204. The Barn is built in the shape of a cross, with ashlar faced buttresses supporting 4ft thick walls of roughly coursed Cotswold stone. The roof is high pitched with rows of oak posts bearing the main load, and resting on stone pillars. Used by the monks to store crops, the history of the barn is somewhat sketchy. After the Dissolution of the Monasteries it passed to the Mores, then later to the Pleydell Bouverie family as part of the nearby Coleshill Estate.

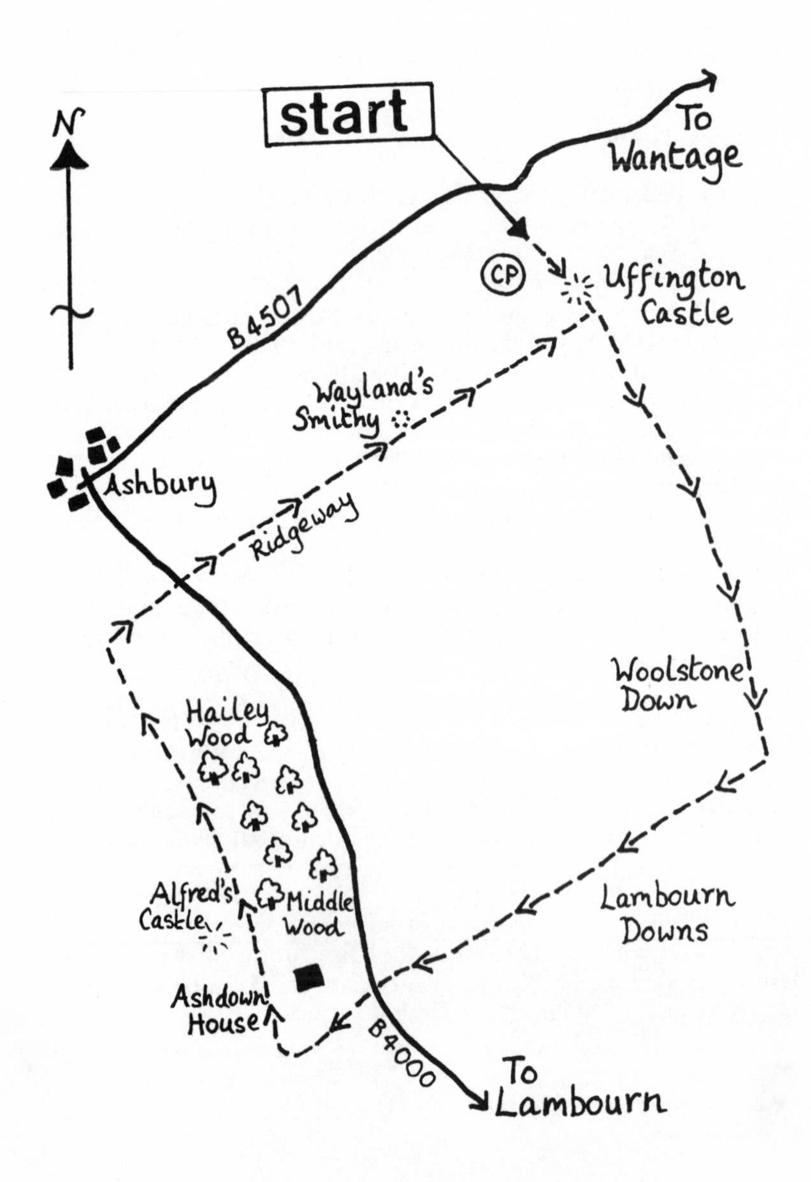
start
N
To
Wantage
B4507
CP
Uffington
Castle
Wayland's
Smithy
Ashbury
Ridgeway
Woolstone
Down
Hailey
Wood
Alfred's
Castle
Middle
Wood
Lambourn
Downs
Ashdown
House
B4000
To
Lambourn

WALK EIGHT

Uffington Castle, Ashdown House and Wayland's Smithy

Introduction: White Horse Hill in the south-west corner of Oxfordshire near Ashbury provides a spectacular starting point to this walk. Overlooking vast sweeps of downland and plain the hill is a popular local beauty spot and landmark rising to over 850ft.

From here the route heads south and then west across the wide open stretches of the Lambourn Downs. At length we reach Ashdown House, an elegant but endearing large scale doll's house looking curiously out of place in its dramatic windswept setting on the chalk uplands. The final leg of the walk is along the Ridgeway path past Wayland's Smithy, a long barrow with a cold and ghostly atmosphere beneath a circle of trees.

It would be best to avoid Fridays when Weathercock Hill and Middle and Hailey Woods are closed.

Distance: The circuit is about 8 miles and should take three and a half to four hours to complete not including time spent at Ashdown House or Uffington Castle.

Refreshments: There are good pubs to be found in nearby Lambourn and Ashbury as well as other villages in the locality. On the circuit itself there are some excellent places at which to stop and picnic.

How to get there: From Wantage take the B4507 road towards Swindon and follow the signs for the main White Horse Hill car park which is located about 2 miles to the north-east of Ashbury.

The Walk: Pass through the gate by the National Trust sign and then cross the field towards Uffington Castle (HN). Cross the single track road and then follow the clear path running diagonally left over the grassy slopes of White Horse Hill (HN). The village of Uffington is distinct a short distance away in the Vale of the White Horse. Just under the hill at this point is The Manger, a steep comb sometimes described as a huge geological gouge in the earth. You can see it quite clearly with the road weaving like a snake below it.

Soon you reach a triangulation point on the right and looking across to the eastern horizon you will see the radio station at Sparsholt. Continue with the walk and make for a stile in the fence up ahead. Negotiate the stile and then briefly follow the Ridgeway by turning right and walking along the ancient track for a few yards. Ahead of you are the Lambourn Downs, a vast immensely spectacular spread of open downland interspersed with distant smudges of woodland unfolding before you like a huge carpet suffused with greens and browns.

Bear left at the waymarked bridleway and follow the track with superb, uninterrupted views over to the right. The outline of a remote downland farm is visible down below you. Keep to the track as it turns abruptly left and then after a few yards pass through a gate and continue ahead along the right hand boundary of the field.

There are splendid downland views to the left of the path now. At the top of the hill draw level with a patch of woodland on the right and just beyond the trees the route joins some training gallops. Continue ahead over the gallops following a path signposted 'Footpath — No Horses'. Keep to the path between the white posts and identify its route by following the arrows. At length, beyond the line of trees on the right, the path drops down gently and when you reach another 'Footpath — No Horses' sign take the second right hand track, avoiding the sharp right hand turning immediately before it and forming part of the gallops.

Follow the track out across the downland. At once the route ahead is clear and visible to the eye for probably a mile or two, the track eventually losing itself in the distant slopes of the downs. This stretch of the walk is noticeably more isolated. Here you are in a still, soundless world enclosed by a ring of dramatic hills and sweeping downland unchanged by the years. An occasional farm building might peep into view but that is all.

On reaching a belt of woodland continue ahead with the trees on your right. Beyond the trees, at the junction, bear left and then after a few yards turn right towards the downland ridge. Pass over a cross track and continue. Maddle Farm is visible over to the left now.

The track here forms the county boundary with Oxfordshire on the right of the fence and Berkshire to the left. At the foot of the hill take the right hand turn and climb to the top to reach a junction of tracks. Cross the field opposite heading towards the stile and the weathercock on top of aptly named Weathercock Hill. From this landmark there are splendid views of Ashdown House in its remote setting amid the downs. Head down towards the road by going diagonally right and aim for the stile. Cross it and here you have a choice. In order to visit Ashdown House (HN) and stroll among the trees of Hailey and Middle Woods turn right and walk along the road to the main entrance. On leaving the house take the drive to the east and follow it through the grounds to the white gate. Turn right at the junction. If the house is closed take the turning marked 'private entrance to Ashdown House'.

When the lane bears sharp left continue ahead onto a cart track. Follow it round to the right and then take the waymarked path for Ashbury keeping to the right hand boundary of the field. There are superb views of Ashdown House on the right, its delicate Dutch style architecture visible through an avenue of well ordered trees.

Up ahead are the remains of Alfred's Castle (HN). Cross the stile on the right and then continue in a westerly direction across a field partly enclosed by Middle and Hailey Woods. The field is cultivated but there is a clear path across it. In a while you reach a field corner on the left. Continue ahead with the wire fence on your immediate left. Gradually the field narrows and at the opening press on towards the remains of Red Barn.

Follow the track between the fields making for a gap in the hedge up ahead. On reaching it turn right onto the Ridgeway and stay with it for some time. The wide track crosses the

B4000 road and continues in a north-easterly direction towards Uffington Castle. In a while thick hedgerows begin to close in either side of the track. Disregard a cross track and proceed ahead. Soon you reach the turning to Wayland's Smithy on the left. Pass through the gate and walk a short distance to a circle of beech trees beneath which is Wayland's Smithy (HN). After visiting the site return to the gate, go left and continue the walk.

Shortly the hedgerows thin somewhat and there are excellent views ahead up towards the finish of the walk at Uffington Castle and over glorious downland either side of the track. Pass over another cross track and continue ahead. Begin the gradual ascent towards White Horse Hill and go forward at a further cross track where there is a signpost indicating 'White Horse Hill ⅓ mile'.

The climb is much steeper now as you approach the end of the walk, the views appropriately spectacular. Cross the stile on the left beside the National Trust sign and walk ahead over the grassy slopes of White Horse Hill with Uffington Castle on the right on the crown of the hill.

Cross the single track road again and walk across the field back to the White Horse Hill car park where the walk started.

Historical Notes

Uffington Castle: Uffington Castle on top of White Horse Hill is a prehistoric fort covering about 8 acres and roughly oval in shape. The monument is enclosed by a rampart and a deep outer ditch.

White Horse Hill: It is believed the White Horse itself was carved into the chalk sometime in the 1st century AD though its origin is unknown. Some say it was intended to celebrate King Alfred's victory over the Danes at the Battle of Ashdown in AD 871. Other sources insist that it was carved as the tribal emblem of a non Belgic tribe called the Dobunni whose territory was this area. At 365 ft long and 130 ft tall the splendid galloping figure of the horse is best appreciated from some distance, notably around Longcot, 3 miles away.

Ashdown House: The house is not typical of what has come to be regarded as traditional English country house architecture. It was probably built around 1665. The architect is unknown but the builder was William Winde who was brought up in the Netherlands and this may partly explain the strong Dutch influence in the design. Tall, ornate and looking a bit like an enormous doll's house it was built for William, 1st Earl of Craven, one of the wealthiest figures of the 17th century. He was a devoted confidant and benefactor of Charles I's sister, Elizabeth, Queen of Bohemia. Craven dedicated Ashdown House to her shortly after her return to England at the time of the Restoration. However, she never lived to see the house and died in London, leaving Craven her collection of portraits, some of which still adorn the walls of the house. Now the property of the National Trust, the house and garden are open on Wednesdays and Saturdays, April to October, 2pm-6pm.

Alfred's Castle: What can be seen today of this Iron Age hill fort covers about 2 acres. The site originally lay inside a much larger enclosure now only visible on aerial photographs. The high banks were once faced with sarcen stones but these have been removed over the years. Many of them were used in the construction of Ashdown House and a number of them can still be seen in Ashdown Park. Pottery finds from the site date from early Iron Age to the Saxon period.

Wayland's Smithy: This site is Neolithic and consists of two periods of construction. The first was an earthen long barrow edged by quarry ditches and covering a chamber of stone and timber containing 14 skeletons. An outer ditch was then dug to supply material for a second barrow roughly 180ft long which covered the first. This second barrow is thus the only one visible today. At the south end of the barrow are six large sarcen stones flanking the entrance to a stone burial chamber. At least eight bodies were interred here. The construction of both barrows can be dated to between 3500 BC and 3000 BC. The monument has been reconstructed in recent years.

The legend of Wayland, the smith of the Gods, is that travellers who left their horses at the smithy together with a silver coin on one of the stones of the burial chamber would, upon returning the next morning, find the coin gone and the horse newly shod by the invisible smith.

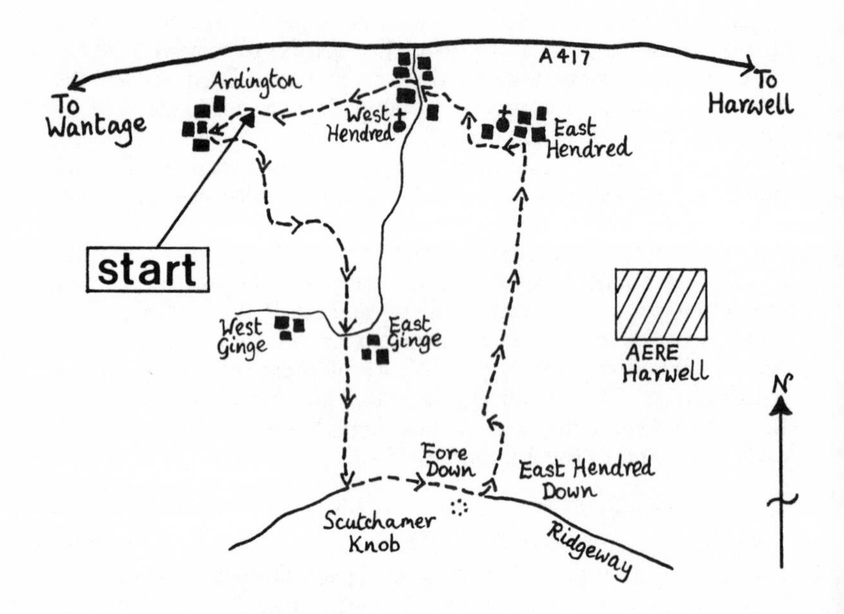
A417
To Wantage
To Harwell
Ardington
West Hendred
East Hendred
start
West Ginge
East Ginge
AERE Harwell
N
Fore Down
East Hendred Down
Scutchamer Knob
Ridgeway

WALK NINE

Ardington, The Ridgeway and The Hendreds

Introduction: The Downs form the setting for much of this splendid walk. Following the historic Ridgeway path over high windswept ground to the burial mound at Scutchamer Knob, the walk then swings north to reach East and West Hendred before finishing at Ardington one of a pair of villages that are part of an old fashioned country estate passed from father to son over several generations.

This is an area with strong equestrian associations too and it is not unusual to encounter strings of horses at various stages of the route. Finally, the scenery on the Downs is never less than spectacular, the views are constant and uninterrupted and the villages offer a pleasing alternative to the loftier expanses.

Distance: The route is approximately 8 miles in length and should take 3 to 3½ hours to complete.

Refreshments: The Boars Head at Ardington offers a simple menu and the Post Office sells sandwiches. At East Hendred there are a number of Inns, some providing hot and cold bar food, morning coffee and Sunday lunches. The Hare at West Hendred serves food and has a garden.

How to get there: Leave the A34 south of Abingdon at the Chilton exit and head west on the A417 towards Wantage. Ignore the signs to East and West Hendred and then after about a mile turn left for Ardington. Follow the road round to the right and make for the car park in the village centre.

The Walk: From the car park in the centre of Ardington (HN) turn left opposite the Loyd Lindsay Room and head along the

High Street passing the Post Office on the left. Just beyond it, turn right into Church Street and follow the road round to the right, noting the entrance to Ardington House on the left and then, a little further along, the village pub, The Boars Head, also on the left. Ardington church lies next door to the inn in a delightful corner of the village full of striking houses and cottages.

The route turns left at the road junction and crosses a bridge on the edge of the village. Once over it bear left onto a waymarked path following it along the left hand edge of the field. Shortly the line of trees on the left gives way to provide a splendid view of the village church and the buildings of Ardington and just across the lake the elegant southerly facade of Ardington House.

When you reach the stile at the junction of tracks turn right and head south towards gently swelling ground. Keep to the track along the right hand edge of the fields and as you approach the junction glance back for a delightful view of Ardington away in the distance. Looking around, you will see that you are surrounded by fine downland landscape so characteristic of this area.

On reaching the path junction turn left and follow a track over level ground. Head down towards the copse and, on reaching the track at the bottom, continue straight ahead onto the little path between the trees. Walk down to Ginge brook (HN), cross over it by the wooden bridge and then climb up the bank on the other side, swinging round to the right at the top to join a grassy path running parallel with the trees and the babbling waters of the brook beneath them.

Keep to the left hand bank and in a while the buildings of West Ginge come into view over to your right. Continue along the path and pass over a stile. Soon you reach the road, no more than a quiet country lane, opposite The Malt House. Turn right for a few steps along the road, over Ginge brook and then swing left along a signposted bridleway. The route passes through a gap between the hamlets of West and East Ginge, just a few hundred yards from each other and then, when the lane begins to sweep round to the right, continue ahead along a straight, sometimes muddy path.

The path lined by bushes and overhanging trees begins a

gradual ascent up through the fields. Shortly the climb becomes steeper and rather more strenuous as you head up into more isolated country towards Ardington Down and East Ginge Down. However, the ascent is not just a breathless, wearisome push onto the downs. Some way up there is a chance to pause and admire the superb views across north and east Oxfordshire. Points of interest are the distinctive cooling towers of Didcot Power Station in the distance and, near at hand, the Atomic Energy Research Establishment at Harwell peeping above the trees. As you climb higher so the views widen to take in a broad sweep of countryside to the west towards Wantage and the Vale of the White Horse.

Before long the path reaches The Ridgeway (HN). Turn left and follow the wide ancient track in an easterly direction and as you cross this high, windswept ground of open fields and remote downland there are good views to the north of the Oxfordshire Plain.

Soon the Ridgeway passes a familiar triangulation point over on the left side of the path while on the right is the entrance to Scutchamer Knob (HN). It is worth pausing here for a few moments to inspect this historic burial mound and walk around its tree-shaded rim. There are some impressive southerly views from here over wood and open downland stretching to the Berkshire border. Head for the junction a few yards to the east of Scutchamer Knob and then bear left away from the Ridgeway. Follow the tree-lined lane as it drops between Fore Down on the left and East Hendred Down and the buildings of Harwell on the right. Further down it swings round to the left and then quickly right before running in a straight line for some distance between lines of trees and banks of scrub. Pass a corrugated barn on the right and continue ahead.

Soon you reach The Ridgeway Lodge Guest House on the left with several houses and a bungalow beyond it. Once clear of this tiny community, the lane cuts between open fields on the left and a plantation on the right. Pass a turning to Oldfield farm and then the road begins to run down between trees and farm buildings.

Enter the village of East Hendred (HN) following a street lined by rows of charming old houses and cottages and with the tower of the parish church clearly visible ahead of you through the trees. If refreshment is your main priority then head for the village centre further along the street passing St Mary's Road on the right, several black and white timbered cottages on the left and a little further on you will find a generous selection of inns.

Afterwards make for the church and turn into Church Street alongside it. Follow the road as it swings first left and then right by a picturesque cottage and at the junction go straight across to join a path running to the edge of the village. At the next junction turn right onto a track and follow it as it curves round towards West Hendred, crossing over a stream by a delightful old mill with the mill race bursting through an archway beneath the house.

Continue along the track between various farm buildings and then swing left to reach a T junction in West Hendred (HN). Turn right here and walk up the road for some distance and immediately beyond Bank Side turn left onto a waymarked path. The Hare public house is a minute or two from here. Continue to the junction with the main road and the inn is opposite.

Returning to the walk keep to the left edge of the field with traffic on the busy A417 road visible away to the right. Looking south from here there are good views to the crest of the downs and the Ridgeway Path.

In the corner of the field turn left for a few yards and then right and now walk along the left hand edge of the next field. Follow the boundary as far as the corner and then continue ahead to the gate along a narrow path between a wire fence and a hedge. Pass through the wooden gate over the stile and then go straight ahead towards the line of trees. Pass between the trees and then cross the field to the next stile. Continue to another line of trees, then head for a gateway with an adjoining stile leading on to a track.

Keep to the track as it passes plantations and then cuts between open fields to reach a row of cottages on the right. Just beyond the cottages join the road on the outskirts of Ardington and turn right. Pass Jubilee Cottages and the John Campbell Gallery on the left and then at the road junction keep ahead. This is the High Street taking you back to the car park in the centre of the village where the walk started.

Historical Notes

Ardington, together with neighbouring Lockinge, form part of a large self contained country estate established in the latter half of the 19th century by Robert Loyd-Lindsay VC KGB (later Baron Wantage) and his wife Harriet, and which remains virtually unchanged to this day. In 1944 the 18,000 acre estate passed to Christopher Loyd, son of Lady Wantage's cousin. To help clear death and estate duties he ordered the Wantage's old home to be demolished and sold 8,000 acres, a number of cottages and many art treasures. Loyd moved to a smaller house nearby. Ardington includes an inn, The Boars Head, a church and Ardington House, an elegant 18th century mansion. The social economic and political climate has changed since Baron Wantage's day but in spite of everything the estate has survived. A reporter from the *Daily News* wrote of the estate in 1891: 'It was a little self-contained world in which nobody is idle, nobody is in absolute want, in which there is no squalor or hunger.'

Ginge Brook: Looking at this peaceful stretch of water flowing through the countryside it is hard to believe that once it helped the villages of East and West Hendred to achieve prosperity. The flow of the brook was such that it powered watermills, not only to grind corn, but to work fulling mills for beating and fulling the cloth which was once manufactured in this area. The brook also played a vital role in the process of soaking flax to make the fibres soft enough to spin.

The Ridgeway: A long distance footpath, 85 miles in length, officially opened in 1973 the Ridgeway path must have been a major east-west route in prehistoric Britain.

Scutchamer Knob is a Saxon long barrow close to the county boundary between Oxfordshire and Berkshire. Its height originally rose to about 77 ft but now it is only a few feet. In the 19th century it was raided by archaeologists but the mound yielded nothing in the way of real treasures.

East Hendred: In the 16th and 17th centuries the village was well known as a centre for cloth and a fair took place annually along the Golden Mile stretching as far as the Ridgeway. Many of the timber-built houses and thatched cottages in East Hendred date from that period.

Hendred House has been in the Eyston family since the 15th century. The family was related by marriage to Sir Thomas More. The 13th century Roman Catholic Chapel of St Amand, adjacent to the house, was pillaged by William of Orange and his army on their way through the village. Close to the centre is the perpendicular Champ's Chapel built by the Carthusian monks. The parish church of St Augustine is 13th century and has been heavily restored.

West Hendred: The church is mainly 15th century perpendicular. The interior has some notable features in woodwork. The font cover, reading desk and pulpit are among them.

WALK TEN

Abingdon, the Thames and Sutton Courtenay

Introduction: Apart from the Thames the market town of Abingdon boasts many historic buildings, some fine old houses and a distinctive church spire which is never far from the walk. As the walk leaves Abingdon it passes picturesque stretches of water alive with rivercraft. After exploring many scenic stretches of countryside, patches of peaceful farmland and the village of Drayton, the walk passes near to the awe-inspiring cooling towers of Didcot power station. Leaving the outskirts of Didcot behind the walk turns to visit Sutton Courtenay, a village of great charm and character. The homeward leg is a pleasant canal and riverside stroll back to Abingdon.

Distance: The walk is about 6½ miles long. Allow just over 3 hours to complete it.

Refreshments: Abingdon boasts many town inns. At Sutton Courtenay The Swan provides hot and cold bar food; the George and Dragon has a beer garden and terrace, and offers coffee and lunchtime and evening meals. The Lion at Culham serves bar snacks and has a beer garden.

How to get there: Leave the A34 at the A415 Abingdon exit and head for the town centre. There is ample parking close to the Market Place where the walk begins.

The Walk: Make for the Market Place in Abingdon (HN) and begin the walk beside County Hall and the Borough Museum on the southern side. From this point proceed along East St Helen Street behind the hall, passing between rows of elegant period buildings and The Kings Head and Bell public house on

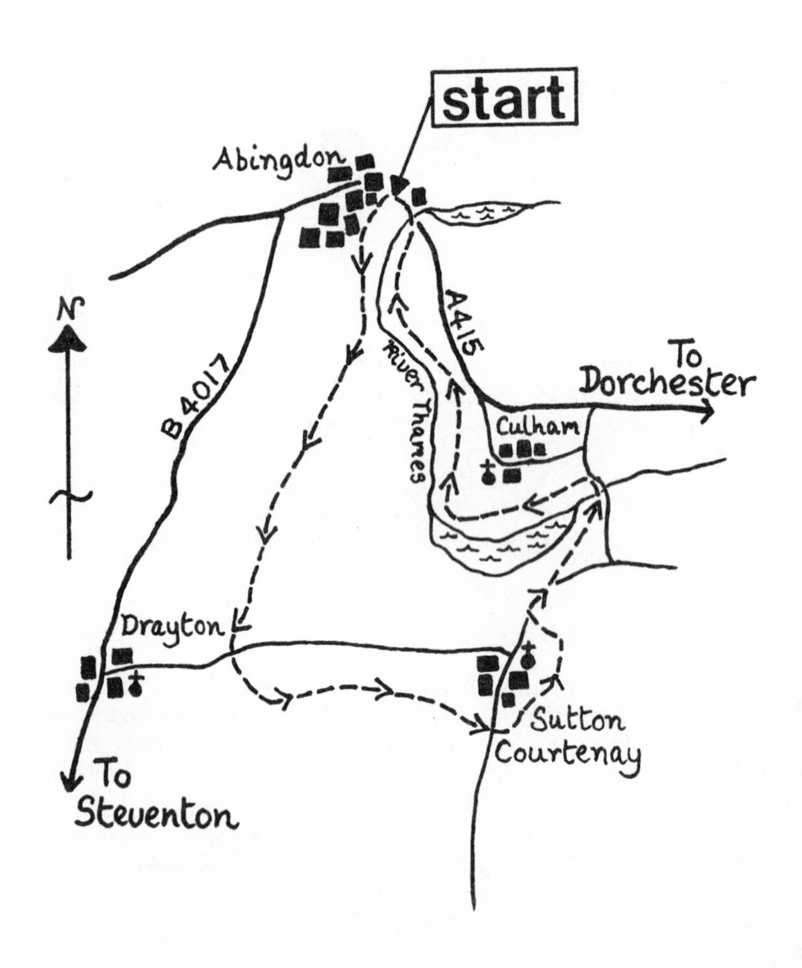
start
Abingdon
N
B4017
A415
River Thames
To Dorchester
Culham
Drayton
Sutton Courtenay
To Steventon

the left. The majestic spire of St Helen's parish church (HN) is visible at the far end of the street.

Pass to the left of the church and then emerge onto St Helen's Wharf overlooking a colourful, picturesque reach of the Thames. There are seats beside the river and this stretch of water is often busy with sightseers, pleasure boats and cruisers. To the left is Abingdon Bridge.

The walk turns right, however, and quickly reaches Long Alley Almshouses (HN). Note the plaque which reads:- 'God openeth his hand and filleth all things living with plentiousness be therefore followers of God as good children' — 1674.

Pass the Old Anchor Inn on the right, cross the river Ock (HN) and then bear left into Wilsham Road. The cooling towers of Didcot power station dominate the horizon but on your left there is a pleasing prospect of fields and meadows. Follow the road as it runs beside the river and in a while you reach the Abingdon Marina development. At the junction of North Quay and West Quay turn right and follow the road round to the left. When you reach the junction with the playing fields in front of you, turn right and walk along the road as far as the right-hand bend, passing the Rugby Club on the left. Cross over towards Metcalfe Close and then head in the direction of the tennis courts, turning right immediately before them. At the end of the tennis courts proceed diagonally left across the playing field to the right-hand corner. Turn right into the field and, with a line of houses visible over on the right, walk along the left-hand edge as far as a gap in the hedge on the left. Pass through it and then over the ditch into a large field enclosed by trees and hedges. Look for the roof of a house just visible above the trees in the far right-hand corner and head towards it. In the corner aim for a section of fence and a gate and then go up the hill towards a pair of semi-detached houses at the top. Cross out onto an unmade road in front of the houses and then turn left. At the next left bend continue ahead onto a rough track. Keep on the track until you reach a stile on the right just beyond some trees and just before a line of telegraph poles. Negotiate the stile and follow the grassy path across the field to the stile in the next fence. Cross it and immediately turn left along the field edge for a few yards as far as the arrow. Then bear right and follow a path running straight between the fields with the church tower and houses at Drayton visible in the distance.

When you reach the junction with the bridle road bear left and follow it to the main road. In order to visit Drayton and possibly stop for a drink turn right here and walk along the road to the village centre. There are several inns providing bar food. Then return to where the bridle road meets the main road and turn right onto the path.

Follow the path over a rustic wooden footbridge with a pretty stream below and proceed between the trees and fences. Pass over a stile in due course and continue ahead along the left-hand boundary of a field as far as the kissing gate in the corner. Pass out of the field onto a track and turn left. After about 250 yards you reach a road. Cross it and continue ahead along the grassy track heading towards Sutton Courtenay and Didcot. Pass under electricity pylons ignoring a path crossing the route further on.

Soon the track reaches the outskirts of Sutton Courtenay, winding between trees and flanked by various types of houses, cottages and bungalows. There is an old mill too, on the right-hand side. When you reach the T junction note the pub opposite, The Plough, with a delightful, partly timbered old house to the left of it. This is the outskirts of Sutton Courtenay, the village centre being about ½ mile to the left. The path, however, carefully avoids the road though not the village centre itself and comes to the charming main street by way of the back door.

Cross the road, turn right for a few yards and then take the narrow path on the left between several houses with a letter-box on the corner. The path runs in a straight line between back gardens until it reaches some open ground with Didcot Power Station a short distance away across the fields, its enormous edifice dominating the landscape at this point.

Bear left here towards some farm buildings and the recreation ground. The church tower at Sutton Courtenay is just visible. Head to the right of a line of trees and then walk along the left-hand edge of the recreation ground towards a brick building. Join a track just beyond the building and then turn right. Follow the track with the recreation ground now on your right. When you reach a track on the left running between fields of crops, take it and follow it towards the trees. Note the farm buildings on the left now. When the track swings round to the left towards them, continue ahead along a narrow path with trees, bushes and wire fence on the left and crops on the right.

Ahead of you now are several modern houses. Head towards them. When the path swings right, go straight on keeping to the left of a fence with overhanging trees on the left. Pass between houses and then bear left at the unmade road and follow it to the village green in the centre of Sutton Courtenay (HN).

This is a most delightful part of the walk. Apart from the green the village boasts a generous smattering of cottages, some of them thatched, some part timbered, as well as numerous picturesque houses and several inns.

Follow the right-hand side of the green past The Swan and the church and then another pub The George and Dragon. Head down the main street of this classically English village passing many more striking houses and cottages. Follow the road round to the right and, when you reach The Fish public house on the right, take the signposted footpath opposite. Keep to the drive as it swings to the right and then cross over the stile. Walk across the field with the hedge on your immediate left and after a few yards, at a break in the hedge, a glorious stretch of the Thames opens out beside the path with the road bridge at Culham just ahead of you. The village is clearly visible across the fields.

Head along the bank towards the bridge. Make for the gate on the right leading out into the road and then bear left towards the bridge. Cross the bridge and then continue over the Culham Cut.

Once over the bridge turn left through the gate and walk along the cut. This is a picturesque stretch of the walk with brightly coloured narrow boats often queueing to negotiate Culham Lock. Pass the lockkeeper's cottage on the right and continue along the right-hand towpath. Soon, at the next bridge, you reach a sign pointing across the field to The Lion public house. At this point a short detour to the village of Culham (HN) is well worthwhile.

Returning to the walk turn right onto the towpath and head towards the finish of the walk. Soon, away to the right across the fields there are glimpses of Abingdon, the church spire and the marina development on the southern outskirts.

Shortly the cut swings right to become Culham Reach. Follow the riverbank path as it heads north now and, on the opposite side of the Thames, the outward route of this walk is but a short distance away to the west beyond the lines of electricity pylons. The main A415 road closes in on the right now as the river begins to curve to the left. Cross a wooden footbridge and here it is worth pausing for a moment to admire the view of Abingdon and the dominant church spire ahead of you across the meadows. As you cross the footbridge note also the stone road bridge on the right and the house with its garden running down to the water's edge.

The path is now over a wide stretch of meadow. Draw level with the marina development and then a stile takes you into the next meadow. The opposite bank will seem particularly familiar now as it forms the initial stage of the walk out of Abingdon. Pass through a gate with the football pitch on the right. A further gate leads you onto a wide riverside path offering very pretty views of the Old Anchor Inn on the other bank with its neighbouring cottages and almshouses in the shadow of the church.

Head towards the stone road bridge with the Abingdon Boat Centre over on the left. Walk up onto the bridge, turn left, passing the Abingdon Bridge Restaurant, and follow the road back to the Market Place in Abingdon where the walk began.

Historical Notes

Abingdon: Until 1867 Abingdon was the county town of Berkshire. Reading then succeeded it and Abingdon moved into Oxfordshire as part of the county boundary changes of 1974. The town was originally developed around its abbey, founded in AD 700 and dissolved under Henry VIII. Some of the abbey's outbuildings still remain, however, including the granary and the gateway. The room over the latter was a prison until the 19th century.

The elegant County Hall in the Market Place was completed in 1682 by Christopher Kempster of Burford, one of Wren's master masons during the building of St Paul's cathedral. South of the Market Place is the Old Gaol built by Napoleonic prisoners of war between 1805 and 1811.

The 15th century spire of St Helen's church soars above the town and can be seen for miles around. The church, which is partly 13th century, is 108ft wide and yet only 97ft long. Inside there are five aisles, a 200 year old candelabra and a splendid medieval painted ceiling in the Lady Chapel representing the Tree of Jesse.

The Long Alley Almshouses comprise Long Alley, Brick Alley and Twitty's. The oldest, Long Alley, dates from the mid 15th century. The diarist Samuel Pepys came here in 1668 and put a donation in the almsbox.

River Ock: The name comes from the pre-Saxon word 'ehoc' meaning 'salmon'. Nearby Ock Street is the traditional home of the Morris Dancers. They elect their own mayor during a special ceremony annually in June.

Sutton Courtenay: Once a Royal Manor until Henry II gave it to the Courtenays, the village has several notable buildings. The Norman Hall dates from the 12th century while the larger Manor House has gables and a splendid banqueting hall with a minstrels' gallery. The 14th century Abbey with its entrance beside the village green, was built on land which once belonged to Abingdon Abbey and was used as a summer retreat by the monks there.

The church is 12th to 14th century with a 16th century brick south porch and a Norman tower. In the churchyard is a tomb to the Earl of Oxford and Asquith, probably better known as Herbert Asquith, British Liberal Prime Minister from 1908 to 1916. Asquith, who died in 1928, had a house in the village.

Culham: A quiet village with the green set apart from the bustle of daily life. It is worth making a detour to see the local inn, The Lion (formerly The Sow and Pigs), St Paul's church which is 19th century, and nearby West Lodge, Culham Manor and Culham Manor Cottage.

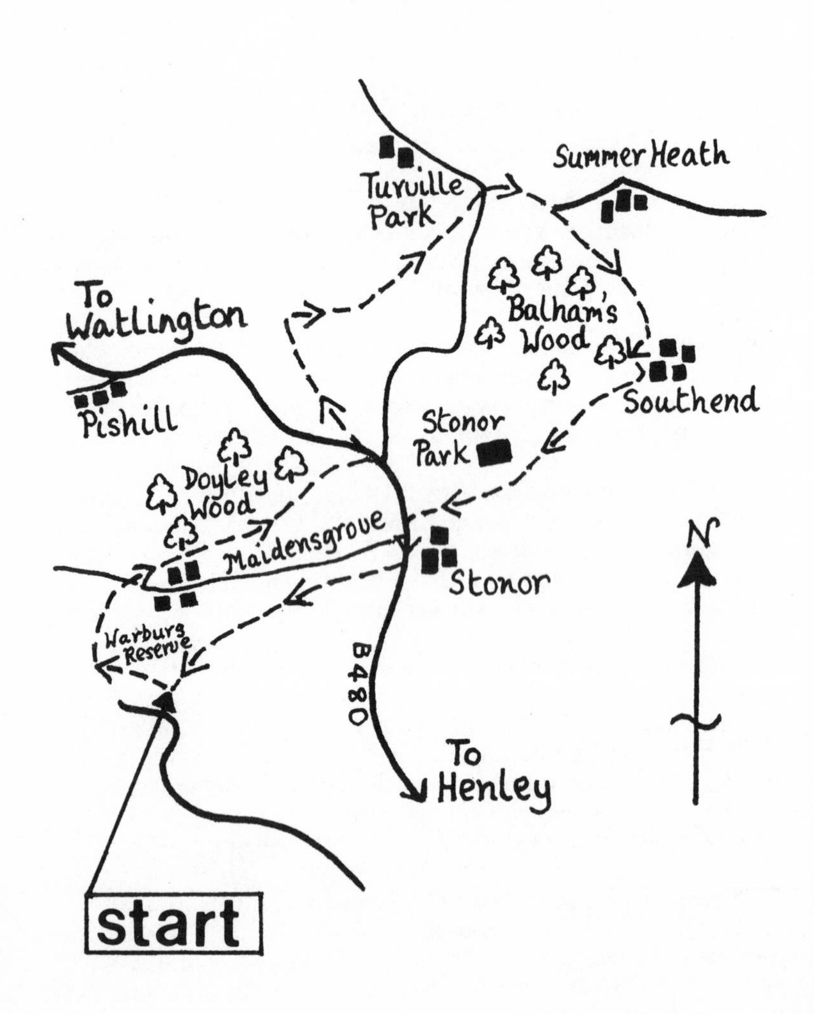
Summer Heath
Turville Park
To Watlington
Balham's Wood
Pishill
Southend
Stonor Park
Doyley Wood
Maidensgrove
N
Stonor
Warburg Reserve
B480
To Henley
start

WALK ELEVEN

Warburg Reserve and Stonor Park

Introduction: The famous Chiltern beechwoods provide a most agreeable backdrop for much of this walk. The route begins by following a nature trail buried deep among the wooded hills. Then it is on to the delightful hamlet of Maidensgrove before crossing briefly into Buckinghamshire and back again. All this is a pleasant preamble, however.

Without question the chief attraction of this walk is Stonor House set in its own magnificent parkland amid the rolling Chilterns. The house and its immediate grounds are open to the public at certain times. The route of this walk is directly through the deer park which is always open to the public. In the park there are constant, unbroken views of the house until at last it is lost from sight.

Distance: The walk is about 7 miles and should take about 3½ hours. Allow longer, of course, for a visit to Stonor Park and if this is on your itinerary it would be advisable to begin the walk with plenty of time to reach the house before last admissions (See Historical Notes).

Refreshments: The Stonor Arms offers bar food most days at lunchtime and in the evening. Booking is essential for the restaurant.

How to get there: From Henley-on-Thames head north-west on the A423 road towards Nettlebed. After about 1 mile bear right onto the B480 towards Stonor. On reaching Middle Assendon pass the Rainbow Inn and then turn left just beyond it (signposted Bix Bottom). At the next junction go right ignoring the turning to Bix and follow the lane for over a mile. When it becomes a track continue along it and then turn right at the entrance to the Warburg Reserve car park.

The Walk: From the car park go forward to the information hut at the far end and then up the path beside it. This marks the start of the Nature Trail, part of the Warburg Reserve (HN). After a few yards, at the junction, bear right and head on up the hill between trees and scrub.

Keep to the path and soon it emerges from the cover of the trees onto a grassy ride. In a while the trees begin to close in again; the path bears left and then right. When you reach Hatch Lane turn right and proceed up the track between the trees. Soon, as you climb the hill, the track narrows to a path with a hedgerow on the right and a glorious view on the left across a generous spread of richly wooded, rolling countryside probably best appreciated from further up.

The path becomes enclosed by hedgerows and quickly joins the road just outside the hamlet of Maidensgrove. There is an inn about ½ mile from here along the road to the left. To continue the circuit turn right and walk along the verge passing Maidensgrove and Russell's Water Commons (HN). Soon a footpath crosses the route; ignore it and continue down the lane.

After a short distance, under some trees, there is a turning to Maidensgrove only. The hamlet is a small assortment of houses and cottages dotted about the clearings either side of the lane. Apart from curious motorists it is a quiet, peaceful place thankfully removed from the bustle of daily life.

At this junction bear left onto a track with a public footpath sign; pass a pond on the left, then a turning to Maidensgrove Farm and continue along the track through the trees. Follow it between several houses and cottages and then at the end join a narrow path, waymarked with an arrow, leading into extensive beechwoods. Almost at once you join a wider path and continue ahead following the arrows on the beech trunks. Ignore the arrows pointing to the left and keep on the path veering slightly to the right deeper into the woodland.

Continue on the main path between the beeches and soon there are teasing glimpses over to the left of splendid Chiltern scenery — beech clad slopes and downland stretching to the horizon. Almost immediately there is a similar vista on the right. Soon the path swings right passing through bracken clearings and descends quite steeply. On this stretch the woodland thins to a narrow belt of trees providing still further sightings of undulating thickly wooded country.

The path levels out and arrives shortly at the B480 road. Turn left and after about 200 yards when the road swings left bear right by a public bridleway sign and follow the lane. The next few hundred yards involve a marked climb between trees and hedgerows and banks of undergrowth.

When, after some time, the trees thin on the right turn right where a signposted footpath crosses the bridleway and walk down the left hand edge of a field overlooking a splendid farmland scene. At the bottom go forward to a line of trees and across a track which signifies the county boundary between Oxfordshire and Buckinghamshire. Once over the track take the path in front of you climbing steeply between the fields.

Proceed up the hill making for a clump of trees ahead of you. Cross the stile between the trees and go through the little spinney. Emerge after a few yards into another field and continue ahead by keeping to its left boundary. Over to the right you can see the thick green carpet of Balham's Wood and down to the right of it the houses of Stonor.

A stile takes you into the next field; this is easy, level hill-top walking. Follow the field boundary keeping a line of trees on your left. Look out for the white painted arrows further on among the trees as you join a track. Keep on the track as it cuts between hedging and fencing and when it swings to the right, go through a wrought iron kissing gate and out across Turville Park (HN) following the direction of the arrow. After a few yards look for a stile in the right hand fence over to the right. Cross into the next field and pass to the left of a solitary tree in the middle of it, making for a stile in the next boundary. Cross the stile, continue ahead, passing to the right of a house and lawn and make for a gate on the right hand side of the drive, immediately to the left of a cottage.

Pass through the gate and walk along the gravelled drive to the road. Cross over it and take the turning opposite signposted Marlow, High Wycombe and Fingest. Proceed along the road and after a few yards pass a turning back to Stonor and Henley. Ignore the turning and continue ahead. All around you is a network of paths and tracks, trees and clearings that make up Turville Heath.

On reaching Summer Heath, a peaceful settlement of houses and cottages, proceed just beyond the turning to Southend and Fawley and then turn right at a public footpath sign onto a path leading into the woods. Keep on the path between bracken clearings and trees. When it forks bear right and continue over a cross track to enter a beechwood. Stay on the main path between the trees and there is a subtle change in direction now as the route swings a little to the right. The path is a little vague and indistinct at this stage but look for glimpses of open countryside up ahead beyond the lines of trees. Make for the edge of the woodland and shortly a stile comes into view leading into a field.

Cross the stile and head diagonally right noting the splendid view of distant fields and woodland and spectacular rolling countryside. After about 150 yards you reach another stile. Cross it and after a few yards notice a white arrow on a fence post on the right pointing ahead. Follow the direction of the arrow across the field. The houses of Southend are visible now. Head towards them along the path. Pass a solitary tree in the field and continue towards the hamlet and a stile visible in the next boundary.

Cross the stile, turn right along a track and at the road bear left. Proceed along the road between the trees and after 150 yards turn right by a public footpath sign and follow a stony track, passing at once a pair of cottages on the right.

Walk along the track between the trees and shortly you pass a turning on the left and on the right. Ignore both paths and continue ahead. The track runs downhill between trees and scrub and in a while a path branches off to the left where there is a white painted arrow on a tree on the right. Bear left at the junction and then after a few yards go right, following another white painted arrow on a tree. Follow the path through the woodland and soon you reach a gate giving access to the Private Deer Park at Stonor Park.

Continue along the main path and when you draw level with the main car park for visitors to Stonor House (HN) over to the right, note the track on the right leading down to it and the admission kiosk on the left.

From the house and grounds return to the main path via the same route and continue in a westerly direction through the deer park with superb views of Stonor House over to the right.

Soon glimpses of the main gates come into view slightly to your right. Pass clumps of beech trees beside the path and very quickly you start to drop down steeply to the road. Negotiate the kissing gate and then turn left. After a few moments, just beyond the 40 mile speed restriction sign look out for a path on the right with a wooden footpath sign pointing the way. If you are desirous of refreshment at this stage of the walk, continue along the road for a few yards as far as The Stonor Arms (HN) and then, suitably refreshed, return to the path.

After a few yards cross over a primitive type of stile and then walk straight ahead across the field passing to the left of a telegraph pole. Aim for the next stile glancing back here for good views of Stonor village at the foot of the wooded slopes. Cross into the next field and proceed ahead following the direction of the white painted arrow. Keep to the right of the copse and note the fine views as you climb steadily into higher country once again.

Continue ahead and make for another stile in the far boundary. Cross it and follow the path into a beechwood. Keep on the path as it cuts through the heart of the beechwood, still climbing gently. At the end of the trees when the path swings right go forward for a few yards to a stile. Cross it and go straight ahead across the field aiming in the general direction of some farm buildings. At the boundary bear left; pass between cottages on the right and farm buildings on the left. Turn right and after a few yards bear left onto a stony track.

Then, after several steps, turn right by a public footpath sign and enter the Warburg Nature Reserve. Head along the narrow path through the undergrowth. The path widens after a few yards dropping down along the edge of some woodland. A little further down you reach a fork with a stile in the middle. Go left and continue down the hill. The path descends very steeply at this point and there are excellent vistas giving glimpses of distant wooded country. Nearer at hand the Nature Reserve can be seen spread out below you among the trees.

Soon the ground levels out and the path reaches the driveway. Turn right and the entrance to the Reserve Car Park will come into view after a few yards.

Historical Notes

Warburg Reserve: The Nature Reserve is named after Dr E. F. Warburg, a botanist who was instrumental in promoting conservation and a Vice President of BBONT (Berkshire, Buckinghamshire & Oxfordshire Naturalists' Trust) in whose care the Reserve is.

The 257 acre reserve consists mainly of ancient broad-leaved woodland with some yew, and later coniferous plantations. The woods and open grassland areas provide habitats for large numbers of butterflies, birds and plants plus 850 species of fungi.

Maidensgrove and Russell's Water Commons: Most of this area was commonland at one time; much of it still remains and is totally unspoilt. Until the Enclosures Acts local villagers could gather firewood and graze their pigs here.

Turville Park: This was once the home of a French Royalist general who lived here between 1792 and 1823.

Stonor House: There has been a house here since the Norman Conquest; the present one dates from the end of the 12th century and has been enlarged and restored a great many times over the years. The Chapel of the Holy Trinity is 14th century and it was here in 1580 that Lady Stonor gave refuge to the Jesuit priest and Martyr Edmund Campion who was later arrested and executed at Tyburn. The house contains an exhibition illustrating his life and work. There is much more to see —sculptures, tapestries, drawings, paintings and many items of fine furniture. There is also the Medieval Catholic Chapel which was in constant use during the Catholic repression.
Times of opening: -
April to September. Sundays only during April between 2pm and 5.30pm. From May Wednesdays, Thursdays and Sundays (and Saturdays during August only) same times. Easter Sunday 2pm to 5.30pm. Easter Monday and Bank Holidays 11am to 5.30pm. Last admission 5.00pm.

The Stonor Arms: The blazonry on the sign is worth inspection. The colours were displayed at Agincourt where Lord Camoys commanded the left wing of Henry V's triumphant army.

WALK TWELVE

Watlington Hill, Christmas Common and The Oxfordshire Way

Introduction: Not too far from the start of this walk in the Chilterns there is quite a steep climb between rows of glorious beech trees to the summit of Watlington Hill, now in the care of the National Trust. The effort is well worth it for there are magnificent views from the top over the Oxfordshire Plain. The delightful old town of Watlington where the walk begins lies just below the hill.

Half way round the circuit is the little hamlet of Christmas Common which apparently gets its name from an incident in the Civil War. The path crosses the Ridgeway and the Ickni eld Way and for a while on the homeward journey it follows the route of the Oxfordshire Way as far as the village of Pyrton.

Distance: The circuit is about 6½ miles. Allow 3 to 3½ hours to complete it.

Refreshments: There is a good selection of inns within the town of Watlington. The Fox and Hounds at Christmas Common provides bar food. Watlington Hill is an ideal venue for picnics.

How to get there: Watlington, about 4 miles south of the M40 (junction 6) and 8 miles north-east of Wallingford, is situated at the junction of the B4009 and the B480 roads. There is ample parking in the town centre.

The Walk: From the town hall in Watlington (HN) turn into Couching Street and proceed as far as the T junction. Turn right along the B480 road, passing Davenport Place on the right, and continue for a few yards to draw level with a

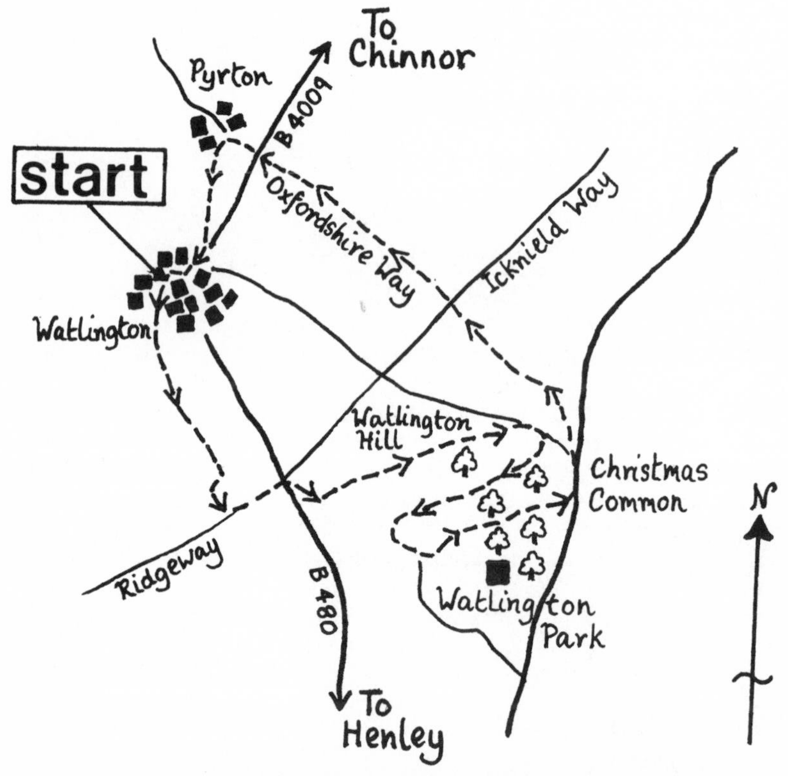

telegraph pole on the opposite side. Cross the road and take the turning marked 'Public Footpath'. Follow the path flanked by walls and shortly the gardens of houses come into view either side of you. On reaching a stile follow the arrow by proceeding diagonally right across the field towards the distant hedgerow, keeping to the left of a solitary lime tree.

Cross over the next stile and then bear left at the fork onto a path between a field on the right and hedgerow and ditch on the left. Shortly the path joins a wide track. Turn left heading towards the wooded slopes of the Chilterns on the horizon.

On reaching the T junction, after about 200 yards with a cattle grid on the left, turn right for several yards and then bear left onto a track indicated by a white painted arrow. Follow the track between a ditch on the left and a cornfield on the right.

Pass a stream on the left in a pretty setting enclosed by trees. Ignore the left-hand path and continue ahead between the fields, the route now following a path.

After some time the path bears right onto a level track with a hedgerow on the left and a field on the right. After a short distance you reach a concrete farm lane. Follow it almost as far as the junction and then turn left immediately before it, cross over a stile and follow the right-hand edge of a field. This stretch of the walk offers some splendid views of the Chiltern Hills, their slopes characteristically clad with majestic beech-woods. In the field corner go forward to join The Ridgeway Path and turn left.

Shortly you drop down towards a house lying at the foot of the escarpment. Follow the Ridgeway path to the junction with the B480 road at Icknield House. The Ridgeway continues on the opposite side of the road heading in a north-easterly direction. Ignore this and bear right along the road, following it for approximately 350 yards, then turn left onto a stony track with a footpath sign. Go forward for a few yards and then bear left at the fork by a brick pillar. The path is waymarked with a public footpath sign. Follow it through a tunnel of trees and foliage as it climbs gently towards Watlington Hill.

After some distance pass over a stile and continue on up the hill ignoring a path on the left. Soon the trees thin somewhat to give glorious views over the surrounding countryside. Proceed up the hill and shortly the path becomes enclosed once more, again forming a tunnel overhead. The route begins to level out now, passing rows of familiar Chiltern beech trees. Go through a kissing gate and continue ahead with a line of beech trees on the right and Watlington Hill car park on the left.

Take a short detour here and follow the path on the left leading into the car park. Make for the opening at the far end and beyond it a path leads to the slopes of Watlington Hill (HN). From here there are magnificent far-reaching views over a sizeable area of Oxfordshire, intricately laid out below you in a patchwork of fields and woodland.

Resuming the walk, head for the road and turn right in the direction of the microwave relay towers up ahead. After about 375 yards turn right at a footpath sign. Go through a gate and then bear right and down a few yards to a wire fence. Go to the left of the fence and along a path, keeping the fence on the right, and a line of trees and some undergrowth on the left. Drop steadily downhill and soon the path is submerged within thick banks of trees and scrub. Underfoot this stretch can be particularly wet and muddy in places. Shortly there are good views over to the right as you reach a break in the trees. Further on the path runs along the edge of a field with distant views of Didcot power station on the horizon. Less than a mile away, to the right of the path, are the beechwoods of Watlington Hill.

Soon the grassy path joins a stony track. Continue ahead along it, passing to the right of some derelict buildings followed by several houses. Keep on the track as far as the junction and then bear left. Almost immediately you reach a fork; take the left-hand branch up the hill to the gate. Once in the field begin the steep ascent towards the woodland at the top.

On reaching the gate and the adjacent stile cross over and, after about 10 yards, bear left following the direction of the white arrow on the tree. Proceed ahead across a small field and as you do so note the graceful facade of Watlington Park over to the right between the trees. On the left the fields slope down towards Watlington. Continue ahead along a level path lined with beech trees. Shortly the path swings right and cuts deep into the heart of the beechwood.

In a while the path curves right. Ignore a left-hand turn, avoid a path on the right and continue ahead between trees and bracken clearings. Shortly the path reaches a metalled driveway; turn left along it passing several houses on the left and then bear left at the road. Follow the road through Christmas Common (HN), passing The Fox and Hounds on the left and then the turning to Northend and Turville on the right. Ignore a turning on the left to Watlington and after a few yards look out for a stile on the left immediately before a sign requesting motorists not to park on the road or verges.

Cross the stile and walk along the left-hand edge of the field. Pass into the next field by means of a rather primitive rustic strip of fence. Continue ahead along the left hand edge of the field, ignoring a path on the left halfway across it. Follow an arrow for the Oxfordshire Way and head obliquely right across the field dropping down to a stile in the corner. Cross the stile and follow the Oxfordshire Way down through the trees. When you break cover there are spectacular views ahead over the Oxfordshire Plain and nearer at hand in the foreground the route of the walk as it cuts between the fields at the foot of the escarpment.

Descend the slope, join a track and continue ahead. Pass a bungalow and an assortment of buildings on the left, followed by the entrance to a timber yard. A backward glance reveals a typical Chiltern scene — richly wooded slopes and rolling hills stretching into the distance.

Cross the line of the Ridgeway and the Icknield Way (HN) and proceed ahead. The track is straight, offering easy, level walking between flat fields and farm buildings. Pass several houses on the right and, on reaching the main B4009 road, go across and continue ahead along the road to Pyrton. Follow the road and, when you reach the village sign for Pyrton (HN) up on the left bank, note the turning immediately beyond it on the left. If time permits a visit to this charming little village is always worthwhile. There is also an inn here at the far end of the village.

Return to this junction and take the turning. Follow the road with trees on the right and fields on the left and, as it swings a little to the right at the end of the line of trees, turn left following the footpath sign to Watlington. Keep to the path as it hugs the hedge on the right. Ignore the path on the right and continue to the field corner. Proceed along the right edge of the cricket field and then turn right by the pavilion. Cross the recreation ground and at the far end join a cinder path as far as the road.

Turn left opposite the Orchard Walk retirement complex and follow the pavement to the road junction. Turn right into Shirburn Street and return to the town centre where the walk began.

Historical Notes

Watlington: The town includes some narrow streets and a number of 17th century half-timbered houses. But the focal point of Watlington is the gabled town hall constructed in 1664 and standing by itself in the middle of the triangular market-place like an island surrounded by traffic. At one time a bridge connected the town hall to the upper floors of the nearby Hare & Hounds Hotel. The church of St Leonard was extensively restored in 1877. The tower is original, standing on the site of an ancient castle.

Watlington Hill: Given to the National Trust in 1941 by the 3rd Viscount and Viscountess Esher, Watlington Hill is a large area of chalk down and copse rising to over 700 ft on the north escarpment of the Chilterns. On the lower slopes of the hill the outline of a church steeple is visible, carved into the chalk. The carving is best seen from a distance and is intended to give the impression that the church in Watlington, just below the hill, has a spire when viewed from the Oxfordshire Plain.

Christmas Common: It is said the village takes its name from an extraordinary incident here during the Civil War. In the Christmas of 1643 the Parliamentarians held nearby Watlington while the Royalists defended the ridge on which this hamlet is situated. Because of the nature of the occasion a temporary truce was called and both armies met on this spot during the festivities — hence the name. Thus the season of goodwill passed peacefully. The church of the Nativity was built in 1889.

The Icknield Way is an ancient prehistoric trade route. Here it merges with the Ridgeway Path but beyond Ivinghoe Beacon in Buckinghamshire it is more of a continuation of the Ridgeway, the old road running as far as East Anglia. With the passing of the years much of the original route has disappeared or has been incorporated into the modern road system.

Pyrton: The splendid Elizabethan manor house here was the home of Edward Symeon whose daughter Elizabeth married John Hampden on Midsummer Day, 1619. Hampden, a leading Parliamentarian in the Civil War and MP for Aylesbury, was fatally wounded at the Battle of Chalgrove in June, 1643. He tried to reach the home of his in-laws at Pyrton to seek refuge but found his proposed route blocked by Royalist troops. Wearily, his life ebbing away, he continued as far as Thame where he died at a house behind the town hall. The nearby church where Hampden was married is originally 12th century but was rebuilt in 1856.

WALK THIRTEEN

Thame Park, Sydenham and Towersey

Introduction: A mile or so outside the quaint old market town of Thame the walk crosses the boundary of Thame Park, a vast parkland landscape scattered with trees and grazing cattle virtually as far as the eye can see. The parkland is dignified, typically English too, with teasing glimpses of its fine 18th century house included for good measure between the trees. On the southern edge of the park, in the vicinity of the village of Sydenham there are impressive vistas of distant Chiltern beechwoods over on the horizon. The walk passes through Towersey with its Tudor and Jacobean houses, before returning to Thame.

Distance: The walk is about 6 miles long and should take about 2½ hours.

Refreshments: Thame offers a wide variety of inns and hotels. The Crown at Sydenham provides bar food as does The Three Horseshoes at Towersey.

How to get there: Thame lies about 13 miles east of Oxford on the A418 Oxford to Aylesbury road. There is ample parking in Thame town centre.

The Walk: From the town centre in Thame (HN) head south-east along the A4129 towards Princes Risborough. Pass the war memorial on the right and just beyond it at the mini round-about by The Cross Keys public house go right signposted B4012.

Walk along the road and after a while, on reaching The Four Horseshoes, turn right into Thame Park Road. Pass over

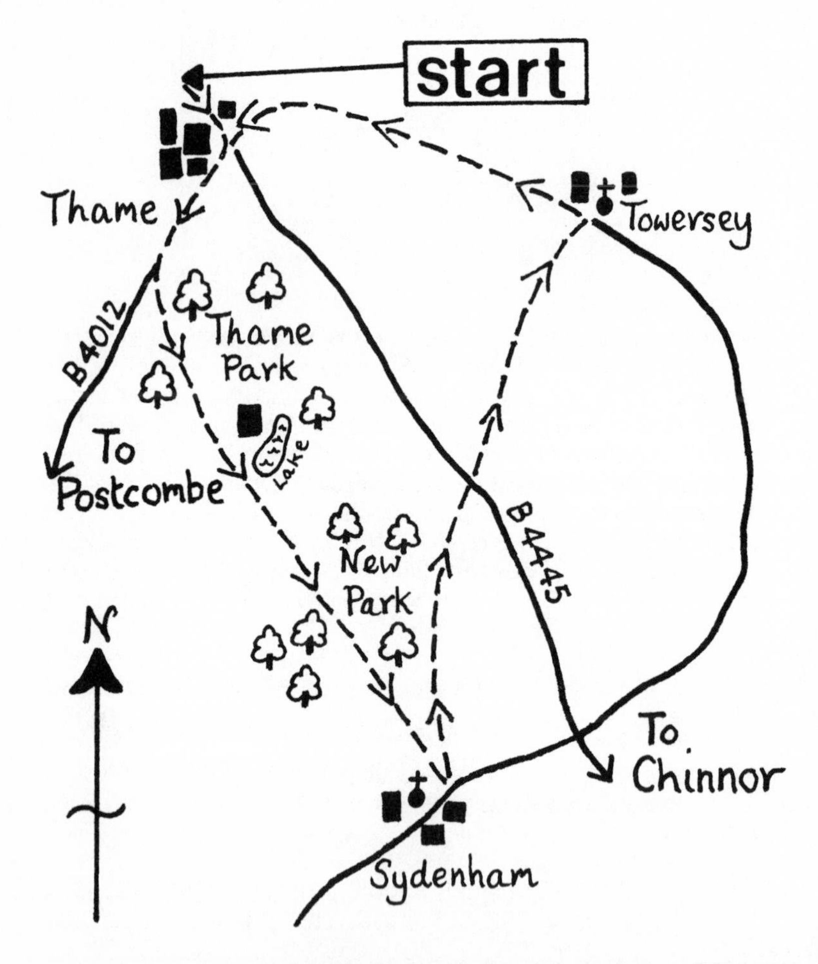

the railway line and follow the road through an industrial part of the town. At the end of the stretch of pavement on the right-hand side of the road continue ahead along the verge over a vague grassy path which peters out quite quickly.

Pass several houses and now the road swings right and then left. Soon it reaches one of the main entrances to Thame Park (HN). Continue along the road for approximately 150 yards and then look for a gap in the hedge on the left with a stile just through it. Cross into the field here and proceed ahead across Thame Park towards the next boundary. However, before you reach it, the route swings right heading in a south-easterly direction through the parkland. The drive to the main house is over to the left now. Continue ahead running parallel with the drive and watch out for a waymarker post up ahead bearing an arrow indicating the direction of the path. Proceed beyond the post and then a second white painted post comes into view some distance ahead.

On reaching the post continue ahead following the arrow, making for a stile in the far boundary. Another imposing set of gates is visible over to the left as you approach the stile. A few yards before you reach it note the clear views of the great house beyond the gates, its graceful façade flanked by trees. Cross the stile, go forward over the drive and then pass over the next stile in front of you, aiming for the next white post a short distance ahead.

On reaching the post continue beyond it in the same direction. The house is still visible over to the left but passes swiftly from sight with every step, screened from the parkland by lines of trees. Head for the field boundary, making for a white arrow in the fence. Cross over the fence then the wooden footbridge over a stream, and pass into the next field bearing diagonally left. In the field corner cross another fence and wooden footbridge over a stream and in the next field head slightly right towards another white painted post. Proceed beyond it and continue ahead, following the waymarkers strategically placed across the parkland as far as the eye can see. Glancing back as you cross this field there are glimpses once again of the house over among the trees.

In the next field corner pass into the next field leaving Thame Park behind you at last. Continue ahead keeping to the right-hand boundary and then in the field corner go through a gate and continue, following the arrow. From here there are splendid views across the slopes of the Chilterns.

Proceed along the right-hand boundary, cross into the next field and continue ahead. Negotiate a stile and walk along the right edge of the next field. Go through a gate and follow the track. At the next gate continue ahead along the concrete track towards the buildings of Manor Farm. Pass between the buildings over a cattle grid and go straight on. The farmhouse is on the right.

The church spire at Sydenham is visible through the trees up ahead. Pass a pair of semi-detached houses on the right and continue along the track as it curves to the left and then cuts between rows of houses and cottages. As you approach the T junction in the centre of Sydenham (HN) you will see Sydenham Old School Room on the right-hand side. The plaque on the wall reads: 'Issued to celebrate 900 years of Norman Heritage. This community is recorded in the Domesday Book 1086. Domesday 1086-1986. Authorised by the National Domesday Committee.' Just beyond it at the road junction notice a plaque in the wall to commemorate the Coronation of Queen Elizabeth II, 2nd June 1953.

If refreshment is of paramount importance at this stage turn right at the junction and walk along the road for a few yards as far as The Crown on the left. Return to the old schoolroom and head back down the lane you followed earlier. After a few yards look for a narrow footpath on the right between two houses. There is a wooden footpath sign pointing the way. Follow the path and cross over a stile after a few yards. Keep on the path as far as the next stile by a telegraph pole. Cross it into the field and continue ahead through the field with trees and hedgerow on the left and the drive to a thatched cottage parallel to you on the right.

Cross the fence at the end of the field and go through the garden of the cottage to the far boundary. Pass into the field and continue ahead towards the next boundary. On reaching it proceed into the next field over the stile. Follow the right-hand boundary and cross into the next field via the stile. Ignore the right turning into the adjacent field and continue ahead with the hedge on your immediate right.

Proceed to within several yards of the field corner and then look for a gap in the hedge on the right and a stile. Cross it and in the next field bear left along the boundary and in the corner swing right and follow the field edge for about 120 yards. Look out for a wooden footbridge on the left and cross it towards the next field. Pass into the field and proceed straight ahead towards the far boundary. Look for a strip of wooden fencing and cross it out onto the B4445 road. Go across to the opposite verge and then take the road in front of you signposted Towersey.

Follow the road between hedgerows and grass verges. Pass a farm, then a cottage on the right and continue along the road as it cuts through level countryside. After a mile you reach the village of Towersey (HN). The road passes under a railway bridge and then reaches the entrance to The Three Horseshoes on the right.

Proceed ahead to the road junction with Church Lane opposite and the village church beyond the trees. Turn left into Thame Road and follow the right-hand pavement. The road runs between hedgerows, virtually in a straight line all the way to Thame. Pass Windmill Road on the right and continue between the hedgerows, the road declining then quickly rising again before reaching the outskirts of Thame. At the busy road junction cross over and continue along Towersey Road. Initially the road is through a housing estate, followed by rows of houses on the left and fields on the right. Walk down to the school and the junction beyond it and bear left. Proceed along the road for a short distance and then turn right into Kings Road.

At the junction bear left into East Street and then walk back to the town centre where the walk began.

Thame: One man has done more towards achieving fame and recognition for this town than any other. He has done much to improve the standard of hotel and country pub catering in Britain too. When John Fothergill acquired the Spread Eagle Hotel in Thame in 1922 there was little business doing. The hotel thrived on market day but only then. During the next ten years Fothergill transformed The Spread Eagle beyond recognition, offering his favourite customers such as Grahame Greene, Evelyn Waugh and HG Wells, a unique and impeccable service. Food was of the finest quality, often brought in specially from abroad. His reputation quickly spread. But conversely he could be rude and belligerent to some of his customers — in particular farmers and commercial travellers for whom he had no respect.

There are a number of other historic inns in Thame and many ancient buildings including some 16th century almshouses and the old Thame Grammar School which numbered Milton and John Hampden among its pupils. The cruciform church of the Blessed Virgin is mostly 13th century. There are tombs of the Quatremain family and an impressive tomb of Lord Williams of Thame, an adroit 16th century courtier.

Thame Park is mostly 18th century and stands on the site of 12th century Thame Abbey. The original building is acknowledged as the third richest Cistercian house in England at the time of the Dissolution of the Monasteries. After the dissolution the abbey was acquired by Lord Williams of Thame. The present house, built by Williams' descendants, includes a number of relics from the abbey.

Sydenham: The village school is mid 19th century and the church mostly 13th century. Restored in 1856 by John Billing the church still boasts its 15th century hammer-beam roof in the nave. Rising over the village is Billing's wooden tower and squat shingle spire.

Towersey: Until 1939 the village was in Buckinghamshire. Now it resides in Oxfordshire, about a ¼ mile from the county boundary. Around the centre of the village are several Tudor and Jacobean houses. The ancient church of St Catherine is mostly 13th and 14th century though it was heavily restored in the 19th century by James Cranston. The impressive Jacobean pulpit is worth closer inspection.

WALK FOURTEEN

Alice's 'chessboard': Otmoor

Introduction: Beckley where this walk begins is a charming village of old crooked stone houses and thatched cottages. The village and its setting belies what is to come, for, a stone's throw to the north-east, the route begins a journey across the wilderness of Otmoor. A curious ghostly stillness pervades these vast tracts of land — 4,000 acres in all — stretching to the far horizon and beyond and noticeably reminiscent of places in the East Anglian fens.

Some of it is sheltered where the walk explores the rural charm of green lanes and woodland. Now and again there are signs of life too — the rifle range, the tiny village of Noke with its pretty church and cottages and welcome inn. But mostly it is a forgotten, abandoned landscape over which the passing years have had little influence. Hard to believe that the centre of Oxford is but a few miles away.

Distance: Approximately 6½ miles this walk should take about 2½ hours to complete.

Refreshments: The Abingdon Arms in Beckley serves bar snacks. The Plough at Noke also does food. Both inns have a garden.

How to get there: Beckley is situated to the north-east of Oxford, just off the B4027 road which links the A43 and A40. Parking is available in the main street.

The Walk: Proceed along the main street in Beckley (HN), passing The Abingdon Arms on the left and, when the road

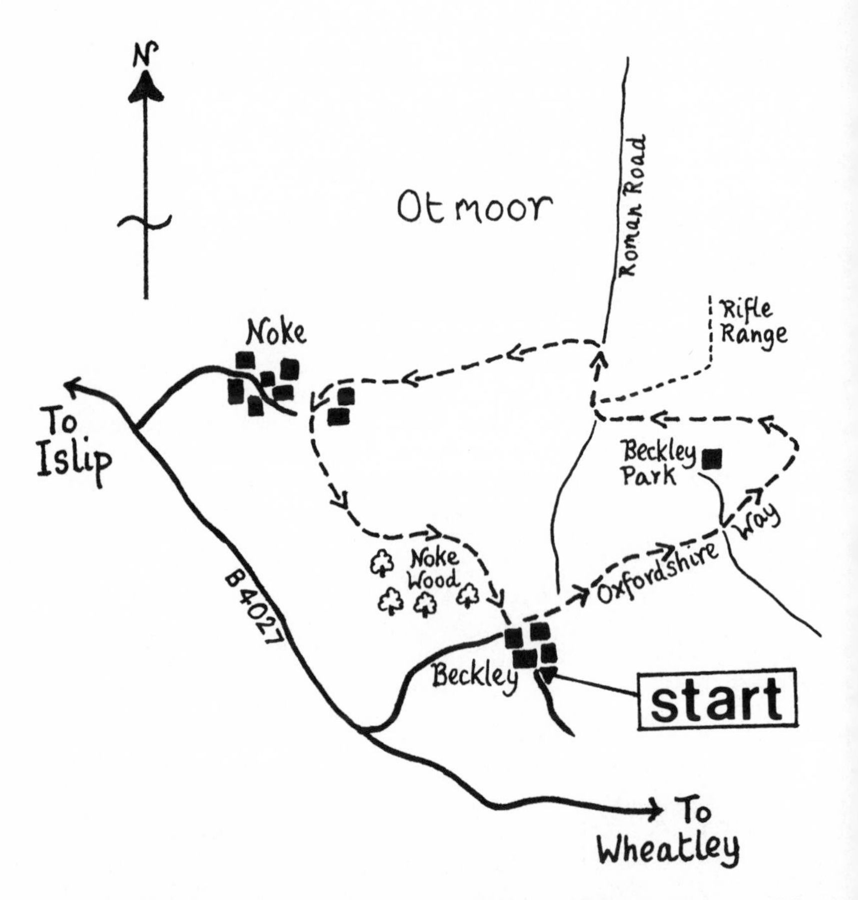

swings right just beyond it, continue ahead along a 'No Through Road'. Very soon the road bears sharp left by some cottages. Leave the road here and go forward onto a shady lane following the Oxfordshire Way up the hill through the trees.

When the green lane levels out continue along it between the hedgerows. Shortly it emerges onto open, exposed ground cutting between fields with sweeping views over distant countryside. Down below to the north is bleak, uninhabited Otmoor, its vast canvas of fields and hedgerows stretching to the horizon.

Soon the track curves slightly right and as it does so, leave it and proceed across the field following a narrow waymarked path, your route still sharing with the Oxfordshire Way. Cross the stile in the field boundary and continue with fine views ahead towards the Buckinghamshire hills. Descend the hillside following the path as it curves a little to the right. Over to your left at the foot of the slope, nestling among the fields and hedgerows is Beckley Park (HN).

Drop down to the field boundary by a copse, cross the fence and then proceed along a level path between the trees with a brook beside you on the right. Cross the brook further on by means of a wooden footbridge and then negotiate a stile. On reaching a drive just beyond it (this is the entrance to Beckley Park) bear left for a few yards and then right through a wrought iron kissing gate following the Oxfordshire Way arrow.

Go forward keeping to the right-hand edge of the field and, after some distance, in the field corner cross a strip of wooden fencing followed almost at once by a wooden footbridge and a second section of fencing. In the next field continue along the right-hand boundary and, on reaching the corner, bear left before a stile and walk along the edge of the same field keeping the hedge on the right.

In the field corner cross over a wooden footbridge following the arrow, through a gate and continue ahead with the boundary on the right. Hug the field boundary as it swings left, at all times keeping the hedgerow hard on your right. In the field corner pass through a gate under some trees and proceed ahead with the hedgerow still on the right. On reaching the field corner turn right and cross a stile in the hedgerow. Bear left and follow the field edge. Take care along this stretch as the terrain here can be very wet and boggy, especially after heavy rain.

On reaching the boundary at last, exit from the field and out into the lane. Pass the entrance to the Military Rifle Range on the right and proceed ahead between hedgerows. Soon the track swings left to a gate. Ignore the turning and continue ahead along a pleasant, sheltered stretch of green lane between trees, hedgerows and scrub. When you reach a wooden gate at the end of the green lane look out for a sign referring to the Rifle

Range. The sign advises you not to proceed beyond this point when red flag or lights are displayed. Fortunately this warning does not apply to this walk as the route heads in a westerly direction here.

Bear left by the sign and proceed up the bank onto a bridleway which follows a dyke or causeway across the southern half of Otmoor (HN). There are ditches either side of the path and the views to the right are over this austere fen-like landscape with glimpses of the church at Charlton-on-Otmoor, known as the 'Cathedral of Otmoor', visible on the far horizon.

Pass over a track and at length go through a gate and into a field. Continue along the bridleway, still with ditches either side. On reaching a path junction turn left over a bridge and head towards some farm buildings. Follow the track and when it swings left continue ahead to the right of the farm. At the junction turn right and walk along the lane passing a bungalow, Hill End, on the right.

Very quickly you are in Noke (HN) and in order to stop at the local inn follow the lane beyond a row of houses and cottages on the right, continue through several bends and past St Giles church on the right and The Plough will be found a little further on beside the road.

From the inn turn left and walk back through the village almost as far as the bungalow known as Hill End and then turn right just before it over a stile with an accompanying Public Footpath sign. Walk along the right-hand edge of the field, following the frequent arrows. At length, after nearly a mile, in the field corner bear left and proceed along the southern edge of the field with a ditch on the right and Noke Wood just the other side of it. At the corner turn right and then, when the path swings left, continue ahead into the woodland following the arrowed public footpath sign.

This stretch is a pleasant shaded stroll between the trees of Noke Wood. Pass over a brook and when you emerge from the wood continue with a fence on the right and undergrowth on the left. Cross a stile after a short distance and enter a field. Proceed diagonally left up the slope making for the next boundary. Enter the next field by means of the wooden fencing and head towards the stile over to the right in the corner. Cross the stile and follow the green lane up the hill towards Beckley.

Soon you reach the village, its pretty cottages and houses lining the road. On reaching the road junction by the church bear left into the main street where the walk began.

Historical Notes

Beckley: Although Beckley lies high above Otmoor it is dominated by the vastness of the plain behind it. In the 13th century the manor of Beckley passed to Henry III's younger brother Richard, Earl of Cornwall, King of the Romans, who built a hunting lodge and a walled hunting park neither of which still exists. After the Reformation the manor passed to Lord Williams of Thame.The church of St Mary dates from the 14th and 15th centuries and includes a stained glass window depicting the Madonna and her mother and some surviving medieval wall paintings which should not be missed.

Beckley has several notable literary associations to distinguish it from other villages in the area. It is said that Charles Dodgson otherwise known as Lewis Carroll, was inspired by the view of Otmoor from a ridge in Beckley to write about the giant chessboard in *Alice Through The Looking Glass,* the vast patchwork of fields and hedgerows, and acres of coarse grass, sedges and rushes giving him the idea. Beckley is also the setting for R D Blackmore's novel *Cripps the Carrier* published in 1877. Blackmore is probably best known as the author of *Lorna Doone.*

Beckley Park: This splendid house was built around 1540 by Lord Williams of Thame on the site of a previous hunting lodge. The present house, encircled by three moats, is understood to be the most complete Tudor house in England. Even its doors and hinges are original 16th century.

Otmoor is a unique expanse of wild, empty countryside that has a strange, haunted quality about it and has been described by different writers over the years as: 'the forgotten land', 'bewitched Otmoor' and 'sleeping Otmoor cast under a spell of ancient magic'.

Most of Otmoor has been reclaimed for agricultural use. Until the 19th century, however, much of it was waterlogged during the year and eventually, by the 1820s, the moor was drained and enclosed as a result of the efforts of local landowners. But this was met with fierce opposition from the local commoners leading to serious rioting. The rioters who came from the 'seven towns' of Otmoor — Charlton-on-Otmoor, Oddington, Noke, Beckley, Fencott, Horton and Mercott — moved in and destroyed new fences, hedges, gates and bridges. But it was pointless. Police and troops were drafted in to help tackle the problem and eventually the rioters acknowledged defeat and withdrew.

In the 1980s the moor was the centre of controversy yet again when for a while it was under threat from a new motorway extension. After much opposition the threat was lifted in order to accommodate a rare butterfly whose breeding ground is Otmoor. In fact the whole area is a paradise for botanists and birdwatchers and there are many different species of birds and plants here.

Noke: There is a charming rhyme associated with this village and its neighbour Beckley.

'I went to Noke and nobody spoke,
I went to Beckley and they spoke directly.'

The residents of Noke apparently had a reputation for being reticent giving rise to the rhyme.

A visit to the church of St Giles tells you that the name Noke means 'at the oak trees' and the earliest reference to the village is 1086. At that time the surrounding area was heavily wooded but today very little remains of the trees. The font at St Giles was given by Gundreda, youngest daughter of William the Conqueror who was also Lady of the Manor of Noke. There is a tomb in the church of Benedict Winchcombe who lived nearby. It is reputed that the figure of Winchcombe, who died in 1623, can still sometimes be seen and heard on cold winter nights leading the hunt through Noke.